Not the Same Person
A journey from heritage to inheritance

Stanley Faddis

All of these stories are true, to the best of my recollection. Many of the names and identifying details have been changed to protect the innocent, as well as the not-so-innocent.

DEDICATION

For my sweet wife, Linda, who has faithfully stood by me from the beginning.

Contents

ACKNOWLEDGEMENT

This book would not have been written if our dear friend Portia Hopkins had not encouraged me to write it. In July 2012, she suggested I start a blog to help me express the pain I felt from the loss of our son, Daniel. I did this and it was very helpful for me to put a voice to my hurt and confusion. After a few months, I began to write about my family, some of who are very colorful and entertaining. I then wrote a little about my college years and subsequent career as a probation officer. Approximately a year ago, Portia said to me it was time to turn my blog into a book about my life, which is what is here. She said she would edit it for me. As she is the head of the English Department at William Jessup University, she is quite qualified for the task. Words cannot fully express my gratitude for her encouragement, guidance and a kick in the rear whenever I need it to keep me on task.

Foreword

The still-Wild-West that is the Online World, as well as bookstore and library bookshelves (albeit in ever-dwindling measure), are awash with authors "sharing" their stories. Sometimes extended, sometimes quite brief.

In the Twitter-verse, the protocol is 140 characters per post. Perfect for our collective now-very-short attention span. The uses of Facebook are as individualistic as each user. Sometimes things of great import or personal interest cross your News Feed (posts from people or organizations you've "friended"). Other times it's an endless stream of cats playing piano or smartphone shots of someone's breakfast.

Politics, advice, score-settling, etc. It's all there in one form or another.

In the early days of the Internet, after communal bulletin boards took hold, the end of the '90's brought the usage and rise of the weblog (or "blog" for short). Again, uses are as varied as each author. For many, writing a blog became a sort of online diary, a writing-in-progress workshop, a way to connect with others likeminded, or to reach those whose thoughts might be far afield from your own.

In many cases, blogs with extensive entries over a period of time successfully morphed into books. And why not? Much of the skeleton of a book was already formed. With a little judicious editing and formatting, a blog could make the transition to a book without the terror of having to start from a blank first page.

My friend Stan Faddis may have had it in his mind for many years to eventually write a book. (It's said that all of us probably have a book inside of us even if we're never inclined to actually write it.) But the blog he started in July 2012 marks the beginning stages of the book you're now about to read.

In this case, though, it wasn't just a matter of Stan finally deciding to haul off and do it. His first blog post appeared one day short of what I expect could be fairly described as the most-hellacious-month of his life after the loss of his beloved son Daniel.

Grieving takes many forms. For Stan, I think there was simply some practicality in getting some of this immediate stuff out and down in written form. But I also know him well enough to guess that his thoughts would never be far from the notion of hoping readers might feel encouraged and a little less alone in reading these field dispatches from his heart-and-mind.

Although this book could never be a true substitute for in-person Stan Hang Time (best accompanied by a fair amount of tacos and diet sodas), it still reads like welcome letters from the dear friend that he is to me.

I found out things I didn't know and he shares many hard-won insights. Not from a place of oneupmanship or a claim to special privileged knowledge, but from a place of humble truth-telling. From a man both broken and yet, against all odds and common sense, still hopeful.

If you're not friends with Stan as you first read this foreword, I can assure you that it's very likely you'll become friends with him just a few pages in. So, now with this introduction from a friend and admirer, it's time to let the man speak for himself. May God bless you as you turn the paper or digital pages.

Bob Bennett
Costa Mesa, California

Introduction

I recall vividly the first time I saw Linda Kay Shackelford, age nineteen. It was in the fall of 1978 and she and her two friends, Susan Bergenholtz and Jackie Reed, were new students on campus at San Jose Bible College. By that time, I had been a student at SJBC for a year and a half. The school's PR man, Mike Maxson, had asked me one day to greet new students as they arrived. As I wandered around the campus I saw these three girls walking toward the cafeteria. My eyes went right to Linda who looked like a goddess. She was tall, had long, curly blond hair and was so beautiful. I made a beeline for them and introduced myself. I asked them where they were from and they said, in unison, "Placerville" [California]. I asked what church they were from and the girl, whom I later learned was Sue, said something like, "We go to the first Baptist, Assembly of Christ Jesus, Church of God." Very funny, I thought. I couldn't stop looking at the blonde one whom I soon learned was Linda. She had beautiful green eyes and an aura of sweetness about her. Although I had dated a number of girls at SJBC by then and had confidence that girls liked me, I felt Linda wouldn't be interested in me and I put it out of my mind to even hope to date her. I put her on a pedestal which was far too high for me to reach.

To make a long story short, we became friends, which was okay with me because I really liked being in her company and figured that was the best I was going to do in the relationship. During Christmas break from school that year, she went home to Pollock Pines and I went to stay at my mom's in Ceres. I should mention that the week before break, I got pretty sick with the flu and stayed home. Linda came over several times to see me. She brought me soup and Richie Rich comic books. We talked by telephone during those two weeks and upon our return to San Jose, she came over to my apartment to visit. I really wanted her to be more than a friend to me, so I asked her to make an agreement . . . for two weeks, she would date only me (there were several other guys who were pursuing her), and at the end of my two-week trial run, we would go our separate ways if that's what she wanted. I was astounded when she agreed and the "two weeks" has now turned into more than thirty-seven years.

However, our relationship was not the fairy tale variety. We broke up several times because I was such a jerk. I was verbally and emotionally abusive and thought I was "all that." I really cannot explain why I was like this, but I was, and to this day I have not forgiven myself for how I acted during our engagement and for the first fifteen years or so of our marriage. I was moody, impatient and sometimes unkind to Linda. She stuck with me through all of it which is such a tribute to her. She is truly a woman of God who displays the fruits of the Spirit like so few people do. To be fair, I have improved much, but I still have far to go. She makes me want to be the best man I can be.

Linda and I were married on July 12, 1980. Sometime in 1996, I told her I needed to confess something to her. We got a babysitter for the kids and drove our VW Beetle to a nearby park and sat there in the parking lot. I admitted to Linda that in 1983, I had had a sexual relationship with another woman who was several years younger than I. As I told her about my infidelity, both of us were crying. I was a blubbering mess as I told her my dark secret that had been eating at me for thirteen years. Before I could ask her forgiveness, she said, "I forgive you." She then said something I will never forget: "Stan, if I had known about this back then, I would have divorced you because you were not a good husband to me. But you are not the same person now that you were then and I'm in love with the man you are today." Her words were so unexpected because I thought she was going to say our marriage was over. Instead, she showed me the same kind of grace and love that God has for us. I deserved nothing less than to have her divorce me. I deserved for her to slap me, yell at me and punish me with her words, but she didn't do any of those things. She simply forgave me. At that very moment, I felt the heavy weight of guilt leave me, never to return. I am hopeful that some of those who read this book will see God forgives us if we ask Him to. He does so in much the same way Linda did for me, without condemnation or judgment, fully and without reservation.

This book illustrates my heritage of being raised in a family, some of whom were aimless and disreputable. Some people would say the Faddises were outlaws. Some of us did not acknowledge the Lord as the Creator of the universe, nor believe that Jesus is the Savior of the world. The primary goal of most of my family members was self-indulgence. They looked for contentment in alcohol, drugs, taking advantage of others, and sex. Unfortunately, during my teenage years, I was drawn to this behavior because it was exciting and made me feel tough so I emulated them. Don't get me wrong: I love my family, but I determined that I did not want to follow in their heritage. I reasoned that if I did follow their example, my future children would follow my lead. I wanted to break the cycle. In rejecting my heritage I have become an heir of Christ and He has promised me His inheritance as indicated in the Bible:

Galatians 3:29 - And if you belong to Christ, then you are Abraham's descendants, heirs according to promise.

Romans 8:16-17 - The Spirit Himself testifies with our spirit that we are children of God, and if children, heirs also, heirs of God and fellow heirs with Christ, if indeed we suffer with Him so that we may also be glorified with Him.

Being a follower of Christ is not always easy, but neither is life without Him. The difference is that Christians who are obedient to God are promised eternal life in heaven as well as blessings here in this life. We will all live forever, but Christians will be with God eternally, whereas others will be separated from Him.

This book is about the change I have experienced and how God has transformed this messed-up, self-centered person into a man He can use to further His kingdom, because I have heard His call and am doing my best to be obedient. I choose the Lord's inheritance over the heritage into which I was born. I chronicle much of my life, as well as the lives of some of the people I am related to and others, including friends and those with whom I have crossed paths. This is my story, but it has much in common with everyone's life journey. I'm not special or unique. I'm just an average guy who, like you, is loved by the Creator of the universe. This humbles me and causes me to hunger for Him.

For years now, I have thought about writing a book. Friends and family have encouraged me to do this. I have felt, at times, a calling to write a book. Why? Several reasons come to mind, including that I have had a lot of varied life experiences, have met and am related to some interesting people whose stories should be told, and I have a keen and odd sense of humor that can be entertaining. But most of all, I have been moved to write because, by 2005, I lost all five members of my family of origin, four of them to drug- or alcohol-related car collisions. Then, in 2012, I lost my son, which I will write about in more detail later. As a result of the untimely deaths of close family members, I am sometimes asked how I handle such tragedies, what helped me escape such an ending; I'm asked why I'm different than all the others. My answer to these questions is because I am a follower of Jesus Christ and this book is our story – my family's, mine and my relationship to God, my Heavenly Father.

In order to help people understand my history and upbringing, I plan to relate stories to illustrate these things. All of us are shaped into the beings we are through the influence of our family, associates, our choices and life experiences. For me, these are not the most positive or healthy of things, but they are my reality.

I am a proud person and am slow to admit my faults, if I admit them at all. But I think, in order for this book to have an impact, I must be very transparent. The man I was earlier in my life, and still am on occasion, is arrogant and critical. This is how I was with Linda; I demanded much of her. I criticized her for not doing things my way, for not being quick to complete tasks such as going to the store, cooking dinner or having my clothes washed. After the kids started to arrive, I seldom lifted a finger to help her. My reasoning was that I provided the money to pay for our lodging, our cars and food for the table. As I have said, I spent much of my time at work, sometimes eighty hours a week, but when I was home, I was not the husband I should have been. Most of the time, I did not attend church with my family. Lots of Sundays, I worked, but even on those Sundays I wasn't at my job, I stayed in bed while she got everyone ready and left the house. As I think back on it again, I am reminded that Linda never complained about it.

Chapter One

As I reflect about my life more deeply, I realize I took many of my cues from my father. He was demanding and expected to get what he wanted in all things. I do not recall him as being a tender man and his temper was short. I feared my father. Writing this has made me recall a story from when I was about five years old. One of the streets we lived on in Turlock was across from a big alfalfa field. Our side of the street had about eight houses on it and it dead-ended at another field. Across the street from the last house on our side was a farm that had a large barn on the property. One day, I was playing in our front yard by myself. I was wearing a pair of shorts. I had no shoes or shirt on because it was a hot Central Valley day. I had promised my mom I'd stay in the yard if she let me go out there. A bunch of neighborhood kids were playing in the water down the street across from the farmhouse. Suddenly, I began to hear loud popping sounds, like firecrackers, from down that way. There was about a fifteen second pause between explosions. The draw of everyone but me having fun and the sound of those explosions was too much for me, so I walked down there to see what was happening.

The popping sounds were coming from the barn so I went inside to find my next door neighbor, Tommy Sexton, Frankie, the kid who lived on the farm, and another boy I didn't know, hitting .22 caliber rounds of ammo with a hammer to make them blow up. I squatted down behind an old stove to watch the action. The next round that exploded ricocheted off something and hit me in the left cheek at the jawline. Blood gushed out of my face and poured down my bare chest as I ran out of the barn toward the kids playing across the street. Tommy's older brother, Gary, put me on the back of his bicycle and took me home. Mom took me to the ER where the doctor put four stitches in my cheek. The entire time, I fretted about disobeying my mom and worried that my dad would spank me when he got home from work. He did. I feared my father but at the same time I loved him.

My father, Harold Eugene Faddis, was born in a cabin near Prairie Grove, Arkansas in 1926. He was the third of nine children--eight boys and one girl. He was called "Gene" by most as well as his nickname, "Wiener." I have never learned why he was called Wiener, but I can guess it was because he was somewhat of a showoff, a "hot dog," if you will. Sometime during the Dust Bowl years, his family moved to California. My grandfather, Leonard Faddis, was a rough man with his children, sometimes disciplining them with a belt across the back, a slap to the face, a punch to the head or by picking up a rock to throw at one of them if they were too far away to reach by hand. Grandpa was also a moonshiner in the hills of northwest Arkansas prior to the move west; not exactly a pillar of the community, nor the type to teach good morals to his many children. This, and his penchant for drinking alcohol, went on down the line to my siblings and me through our father.

Dad was a depression-era child and his family had to scrape for everything they had. Because Dad passed away when I was eleven years old, my life was somewhat the same because we did not have a very good income and my mom could not provide for us many of the things she wanted to give us. She raised us on Dad's Social Security and Veteran's pension. This, as you can imagine, was not very substantial. After I got into high school, she went to work part-time as a teacher's aide at an elementary school where she worked for fourteen years. If my dad were alive today, I'm pretty sure, had he not been injured in the car crash that left him paralyzed, he would have worked in construction until he retired. He was forty-two when he died so he would now be eighty-seven years old. I'm not sure if I think he would have been a churchgoing man. Very few of his seven brothers or his parents were Christians and he was not raised that way.

When my father was about thirteen years old, the family lived near the Susanville River. Lots of people swim in the river in the summer. One day, a couple of my uncles were swimming with two girls who lived close by. They had all taken off their clothes before they went into the water. None of the kids were more than ten years old. The father of the two girls went looking for them and saw them swimming with the Faddis boys in the river and it made him angry so he threatened them with a shotgun. They ran home and got my dad, who was their elder brother, and he went down there. He threw an empty bottle at the old man, striking him in the head. For his crime dad was sent to the Preston Institution for Boys in Ione, California, a very tough reform school where my father learned how to fight.

Dad was not the only kid in his family who at one time or the other got on the wrong side of the law. My uncle Dick beat up a police officer in Susanville and ended up going to prison. After his release, he violated parole for various reasons and was sent back to prison several times. My uncle Carl wrote bad checks and went to jail for his crimes. As an adult, my father landed back in jail for unknown reasons in Merced, California, which is where he was while he was dating my mother. Somewhere in my stuff I have letters they wrote to one another while my dad was in jail. My guess is that most of my father's brothers spent some time locked up due to fighting, drunk driving or a variety of petty crimes.

Then there were the unlawful things they did for which they were not caught. These include selling a stolen chainsaw to a timber faller in a bar who put it in his truck and then went back into the bar to continue drinking. The Faddis boys then stole the chainsaw out of his truck and went on to the next bar to sell it again, doing this several times in a single night. Some of them were adept at plucking cash from the shirt pockets of other drunks in the bars they frequented.

I could've easily followed in my dad's footsteps and been like him. He taught me, through his behavior, to be what he believed a man should be, and I wanted to please him. I'm relieved I did not have him around to continue this lesson plan. My dad did teach me how it is important for man to provide for his family; he was a hard worker and was always employed. He never came right out and said this but I learned it from his example. When I was about seven years old, Dad built me a shoeshine kit out of pine wood. He put all the typical items in it including cans of shoe polish, brushes for cleaning and applying the polish, as well as buffing rags. Using a wood-burning wand he wrote "10 cents" on each side of the kit. He then took me down to the barbershop where we got our haircuts and made an arrangement with the owner for me to come in on Saturday mornings to offer the barber's customers a shoeshine. I was usually paid more than ten cents for a shine even though I got polish on the clients' socks just about every time.

As for Dad's carousing, I didn't know a lot about him chasing other women until years after he passed away when my mom finally opened up and told me some things she had had to live with. I can honestly say I am ashamed of him for treating her the way he did. I don't think he was physically abusive but certainly he was emotionally abusive and his cheating on her made her feel sad and unloved at times.

He was a veteran as a result of being drafted into the U.S. Army during World War II. While in the Army, Dad lost the middle finger on one of his hands. The story goes that he was cleaning his .45 caliber sidearm when it went off and shot him in the finger. Recently I learned from my dad's only living brother, Jim, Dad may have intentionally shot off his finger so he could get out of the Army. Whatever the cause, Dad was left with a hand that, when balled into a fist, was nothing less than a weapon that served him well as he participated in one of his favorite pastimes – bar fighting. Dad and his brothers loved going to honky-tonks where they drank booze, played guitars and sang to entertain the other patrons, chased women, and most of all, fought other tough men who were there to do the same. Dad's hand was given a name. It was referred to as "Ol' Crip." I have never been told why, but I suppose it was either because it was crippled or because he used it to "cripple" his opponents.

There are many stories I have heard about his prowess and skill as a bare-knuckles fighter. The most memorable one occurred around 1957 shortly after I was born. We had just moved to Turlock, California from Redding, California where I was born. Upon arriving in town, my Dad began to ask around about who was considered to be the toughest man in Stanislaus County. The answer was always, "Manuel Victor." My dad wanted to know this information because it was his goal to be known as the toughest which could only be accomplished by besting up Victor in a bar fight. Don't ask me why, but that's what he aspired to.

One Saturday night, Dad went down to the 99 Club where he knew Manual Victor hung out. Victor was the president and leader of a local outlaw motorcycle club called the Bar Hoppers. He walked into the barroom, which had a lot of Harley Davidson and Indian motorcycles parked out front. The story goes that Dad sat down at the bar and the bartender asked him, "Can I help you?" Dad responded by saying, "Yeah, my name is Gene Faddis and I'm here to kick Manual Victor's a**." Victor just happened to be sitting next to my father, heard the comment and immediately took him up on the offer. They walked to the dance floor and were quickly in the center of a large group of the Bar Hoppers who formed a boxing ring of sorts. The end result was my dad beat and bloodied Victor and, in turn, Victor's "right hand man" who was, as tradition dictated, the president's bodyguard.

From that day forward, my father proudly wore the unofficial crown of the "Toughest Man in Stanislaus County." He took on all comers, and there were many. Manual Victor took the defeat very well. He tried to get my father to join the club and be his new right hand man, offering to build my dad a motorcycle. Dad was not interested in being a "biker" and never joined up, but he ran around with them.

Another time, Dad was playing a guitar in a bar for his own amusement. A sailor in uniform came in and, after a while, he told my dad to knock off the playing. I've heard recordings of my dad playing and singing, so I can imagine why the sailor wanted him to stop. Dad kept playing and the sailor demanded several more times that he desist. Finally, the navy man walked over to my dad and stood over him as if to intimidate Gene Faddis. Dad stood up and swung the guitar at the other man, knocking him out cold. Then he stood there with his foot on the unconscious guy's chest and continued to play.

When I was born on April 2, 1957, my father went to a bar in Redding he knew well – Stan's Place, his favorite beer joint. All of his buddies congratulated him and bought him drinks. Someone asked him the name of his new son. Dad explained he and my mother had not yet picked one. The owner of the place laid a hundred-dollar bill on the bar and said he would give it to my dad if he named his son after the owner. Thus, I was christened Stanley Eugene Faddis. I'm certain that hundred dollars never left the bar.

My dad was tough and he was determined that all three of his sons would also be tough. It was important to him that we lived up to the reputation of our last name. Around the towns of Ceres, Turlock, and up north in Susanville, where he and his brothers had grown up, the name Faddis was synonymous with being able to whip everyone we fought. He told my brother Jeffrey and me that if he ever heard of us backing down from a fight, he would whip us. He also discouraged our losing a fight no matter how big the opponent.

One thing I can say for my father and his brothers that they passed down to us is their fierce loyalty to one another. However, this loyalty did not always bode well for whomever crossed them. Dad worked at his construction job from 7:00 a.m. to 3:30 p.m. Monday through Friday. He sometimes stopped off at a bar in Ceres named Doug's Den on his way home from work. One afternoon around 4:00, he was drinking at Doug's when he got into a fight with a guy whose three buddies jumped in and the four of them beat my dad very badly. He got away and went home where he called two of his brothers in Susanville, California. My two uncles (Jim and Dick) immediately jumped in a car and made the five-hour drive to Ceres in just over three hours. By then it was only about 8:00 p.m. and the three of them went back to bar where the four men, who were still there drinking, had the misfortune of meeting my dad and his brothers. Those guys barely made it out of the bar alive but not before being punched, slapped, stomped and beat with pool cues. Such incidents were not uncommon in the world of the Faddis boys and they reveled in their superiority in barroom melees.

As a result of my father's notoriety as a brawler, the name "Faddis" was well known in Turlock and Ceres because this is where my dad frequented the bars and fought. Apparently, his infamy lasted for some time after he passed away in 1968. One evening around 1970, a man came to our front door with his son in tow. My mother answered his knock. The boy had a black eye and two fat lips. The man was quite agitated. He told my mother that her son had beat up his son at school earlier that day and he wanted her son punished for it. My mom said she had three sons and asked to know which one it was. The man looked down at his son and said, "Who did this?" The boy said it was Jeff. Mom turned her head and yelled, "Jeffrey Bert Faddis, get in here now!" At that point, Mom, later recounting the story, said the man's face went white. He said, "Ma'am, did you say your last name is Faddis?" She acknowledged that it was and the man said, "I am so sorry to bother you! Let's forget the whole thing." He grabbed his son and dragged him back to their parked car. She heard the man tell the boy, "Are you crazy for getting into a fight with a Faddis? If I've told once, I've told you a hundred times, you do not mess with the Faddises!"

Another thing Dad was popular for was that he would break bottles over his own head to get a laugh and reaction out of people. I saw him break many bottles this way including beer and soft drink bottles. He could even shatter those thick, spiral Pepsi bottles in this manner. Many times he got cut on his scalp and his head looked like a road map from all the scars. Over his lifetime, it is likely that he broke hundreds of bottles on his skull. I do not know why or how he started doing this, but the crowd he ran with loved it and my dad bathed in the attention it got. Gene was the life of every party.

In 1966, my father was working for a construction company that was building the California Aqueduct canal. At that point, the crew was working near Firebaugh, California. My Dad worked all week there, staying in a motel near the worksite, and came home after work each Friday. In August, Dad stopped off at the local bar after quitting time and got drunk before driving the eighty miles back home to our house in Ceres, California. Somewhere near Fresno, he crashed his old station wagon. A twelve-pound sledgehammer in the back of the car slid up and hit my father in the back through the seat. The sledge crushed several of his lower vertebrae, severing his spinal cord in the process. As a result, my once very active, strong and virile father lost the use of his legs; he was rendered a paraplegic.

I was nine years old when Dad got hurt and I have several memories of him during the next two years. He was in and out of Veteran's Affairs (VA) hospitals where attempts were unsuccessfully made to repair the damage to his spinal cord. During the time he was home, he spent most of that time in a hospital bed in one of the bedrooms. I often slept next to him on the floor on a pallet because I loved him so much and wanted to be as close to him as possible. Being the oldest of four siblings, I felt like I needed to help my Mom care for my father in whatever way I could.

One of those ways was to sometimes help him out of bed and into his wheelchair and then into the bathroom to bathe and assist with his bowel movements. Even then, I was big and strong enough to lift Dad out of his chair and get him into the bathtub. I would then press on his lower abdomen to force the excrement out, after which I cleaned it out of the tub, threw it in the toilet and helped him to wash up. Afterwards, I got him back to his bed and we went on with our day. Doing this for Dad did not faze me at all and I was proud to help him, but now, as a man, I understand how humiliating this must have been for him.

Another memory recalls Dad's independence and his refusal to just lie in that hospital bed. One time when all of the kids were at school and Mom was gone somewhere, he got up, wheeled himself outside and took a shovel and one of the handsaws from his toolbox. He sawed off the handle of the shovel to about a three-foot length, got into our family car, which had an automatic transmission, and used the shovel handle to operate the brake and accelerator pedals. Dad spent the day driving around the county, sightseeing and looking up several friends who were undoubtedly surprised to see Gene driving around in a car all by himself!

In November 1968 Dad was at the Long Beach, California VA hospital following a third operation to repair the damage and to help relieve the pain he almost constantly suffered from the injury. It did not work. In order to relieve the pain, the doctors had prescribed morphine to help Dad cope. On the evening of November 20, he called us from his hospital bed and talked to each one of his four children and then Mom. He said he loved us and to be good--the usual things a father might say to his kids. We were planning to go see him at Christmastime during our break from school, so we also talked about that. We learned the next day that after ending the phone call, Dad went to sleep. Approximately a half hour later, he took a deep breath and died from a massive coronary. He was forty-two years old. I was eleven.

After I got older, I began to wonder how a man who had been so physically fit could die of a heart attack at such an early age. I now wonder if Dad took his own life by saving up a handful of morphine and, after telling each one of his children he loved them and to "be good," swallowed the drugs and went to sleep forever. As I stated earlier, having to be cared for in the manner that was required must have been very humiliating for him. Facing the fact that the surgeons could not fix him, the constant pain he suffered, and the prospect of coming home to be taken care of by his wife and kids may have been too much for him to bear. I just don't know. After this, Mom was faced with caring for her four children, ages eleven, ten, eight, and six. Her income was from Dad's Social Security and Veteran's pensions – approximately $400.00 a month. We lived in a Housing Authority (HA) residence, a four bedroom, one-and-a-half bath for which our rent was about $65.00 a month in 1968.

Over the years, I have compared myself as a father to my own father. We are very different men. While he taught me to fight at the drop of a hat and defend the Faddis name, I did not do that with my son. One way in which we are the same is that we both held steady jobs and provided for our families. As I have written here before, my dad spent very little time with his family because he was either at work, fishing in a nearby river or lake, or out chasing around in the bars on weekends. I do have some good memories of him taking us fishing and hunting. One really nice memory is the time we all went to Yosemite. But those are very few and far between. My father was not an educated man and probably only made it through primary school. I was different in this way in that I achieved a college degree. I believe my dad would have been proud of me for this accomplishment but I think he would have been disappointed in me in other ways. He was a carpenter and likely would have wanted me to follow in his footsteps. I was also not the barroom fighter he was. His "hobby" was drinking hard and going bare knuckles with anyone who challenged him. Think of Clint Eastwood in the movie *Any Which Way but Loose* without the orangutan, and you'll get a good idea of him.

The silver lining in the cloud here is that, shortly before his death, a preacher came to visit my dad and told him the Gospel Story. He accepted Christ into his heart and asked to be forgiven. I believe I will see Dad in heaven and he'll have a chance to say he is proud of me for being the man I am today.

My mother, Delores Lee Taylor, was born in Pearson, Oklahoma, on February 1, 1935. She was the second child in a family of three girls and one boy. I know very little about my mother's growing up and less about how she met my father. She graduated from Turlock High School in 1953 and was a member of a singing group there called the Madrigals. Mom had a beautiful voice and I have fond memories of hearing her sing. One of my favorite memories was her rendition of "Tammy," which had been made popular by Debbie Reynolds in 1957.

When I was about ten years old we went to see my dad in the VA hospital in Long Beach. It was 1967. I was traveling with my Mom, aunt, two brothers and our sister to see him. We were driving down Highway 99 in the hot Central Valley of California from our home in Ceres. As we were stopping to have some lunch at one of those hamburger places that were housed in a huge orange-shaped building, the song "Can't Hurry Love" by The Supremes came on the radio. Mom turned up the volume and sang along with it. After it finished, she said, "I love that song so much!" I'll never forget that moment, and every time I hear that song, I am reminded of that moment in my young life. I miss my Mom so much.

After Dad died, Mom, who was thirty-three years old at the time, did not have it easy. She raised her kids the best she knew how, but I know it was difficult. Foremost, she had three sons who had been taught to be tough, even to the point of meanness. She possessed a high school education and a cosmetology degree, neither of which helped much as she had relied on my dad to handle the discipline. When necessary, she wielded a two-inch-wide belt across our backsides. There was never any doubt that she loved us as much as any mother could possibly love her children. To me, she was the greatest mom in the world.

After high school, my mom went to Adrian's Beauty College in Turlock to become a beautician. She spent some time after this working in the trade but it was before I was born and I don't know much about it. What I do know is that when I was seven or eight, she taught me how to give her a pedicure, which I did often up until I left home for college at age nineteen.

The routine she taught me never changed. She would sit in her chair in the living room as I filled a plastic basin with warm water and put in a packet of Johnson's Foot Soap. I spread a towel in front of her and laid out the clippers, cuticle scissors, file, cuticle pusher, a pumice stone and a tube of cuticle softener. Then I'd bring in the basin of water for her to soak her feet for ten minutes, after which I washed and dried them. As I lay on my belly on the floor, I would clip her nails, apply the cuticle softener, push back and cut off the excess cuticles. If necessary, I'd use the pumice stone on her callouses and then rub lotion on her feet. She loved the pedicures and I loved doing it because I adored my mom and wanted her to feel good. Not long before she died, when I was forty years old, I gave her one last pedicure and I still remember the look on her face as I went about my work.

Mom was a smoker, something she did as far back as I can remember. She smoked unfiltered Pall Malls, but later switched to something like filtered Virginia Slims, I think. I didn't like it because I knew it might eventually kill her. I also didn't appreciate smelling like cigarette smoke, but there was no way around it. She smoked all the time: in the house, in her car, everywhere. Sometime in the late 1980's, Mom had a heart attack and landed in the hospital. She quit smoking, cold turkey. The day of the heart attack was the last day she ever smoked a cigarette.

Mom had other health problems as well. She was an insulin-dependent diabetic and suffered from congestive heart failure (CHF). In 1997 she fell and broke her hip. She was never physically the same after that. The doctors put a huge lag screw in her hip so that the break would fuse back together. After a couple of weeks, she was transferred to a rehabilitation hospital where, during her stay, two male nurses re-broke her hip as they attempted to catheterize her. Don't ask me how they accomplished that. The result was her return to the hospital where she had to be in traction for a few weeks. She was then sent to several other rehabs and continued to decline. On October 28, 1997, Mom died of congestive heart failure in a convalescent hospital in Turlock. It has now been almost eighteen years since Mom passed. I miss her deeply but I rest assured knowing that she is in heaven with my dad, her other three children, and my boy, waiting for me.

In the summer of 1970, between the seventh and eighth grades, Mom took our family on a vacation to visit my Dad's brother, Tom, and his family. I believe that, by this simple act, she was trying to provide a "normal" childhood for her kids. Uncle Tom was a logger and earned a good living as a timber faller. He lived with his wife Rosie and their children, Tommy, Kenny and Tina, in Happy Camp, CA. The population of their town was under one thousand, and it is located west of Yreka on Highway 96 in a remote area near the Klamath River. That vacation was one of the most fun and exciting things our family had ever done.

Several of those days, Mom and Aunt Rosie took all of us kids to a great swimming hole on the Klamath River. We took a picnic lunch and spent the entire day there. We went swimming, explored up and down the river and skipped rocks on the water. Someone had tied a two-by-four-foot board to a tree branch hanging over a swift area of the river. It had a rope handle attached to it so one could stand on the board, hold onto the handle and "surf" the river. It was so fun.

However, the most exciting part of that vacation for me was the day Uncle Tom took me to work with him in the woods. He woke me up at 5:00 a.m. and told me to get dressed. I was a big kid even then and was able to wear his old boots and blue denim work shirt. He handed me some suspenders and an aluminum hard hat, and my work ensemble was complete. Aunt Rosie packed us a big lunch and plenty of water. She gave Uncle Tom his thermos of coffee and we headed up the mountain in his old pick-up to the lumber company landing.

Uncle Tom was assigned a certain section of the forest at an elevation of seven thousand feet in which there were trees marked by red paint. These were the ones he was expected to fell and he quickly got about his business. He gave me some safety instructions including to always stay behind him and to watch for rattlesnakes. He warned me to never step to a spot that I could not see such as over a log as there might be a snake resting there.

Uncle Tom had two chainsaws. One was big and used for cutting down the trees. I estimated the bar on which the chain blade revolved around was four to five feet in length. His other saw was smaller and used for "bucking" the trees. Bucking is when a timber faller walks on top of the fallen tree, cutting the limbs off the topside and both sides so the crew could drag the tree to the landing at a later time using huge chains and heavy equipment. I was fascinated by how quickly he worked. In addition to his saws he also had gas and oil cans, an ax and several wedges. The wedges were made of yellow plastic that he sometimes had to use to finish the job of bringing down the tree, some of which were seventy to eighty feet tall and six feet in diameter. Uncle Tom began by deciding which way he wanted the tree to fall. He had to make certain his tree fell between the others and did not hit other trees. He would then make his first cut on that side of the tree, perpendicular to the ground approximately three feet from the forest floor. The second cut was made above the first one at thirty degrees so that it angled down into the first cut. He then took his ax and with the back of it, knocked the wedge of wood out of the cut. On the opposite side, he made another perpendicular incision, called the back cut, moving toward the front cut. Usually when he got a couple of feet in, the tree would begin to fall. At this time he backed up quickly, never turning away from the tree and closely watching its fall. He always made sure I was a good twenty feet away from the tree before he began his back cut. He had explained to me earlier that one never turns his back on a falling tree, especially in forest as dense as we were in. There was a danger of a limb from a falling tree breaking off as it fell and catching on a standing tree. This limb could later fall on top of you. These were called "widow makers" for good reason.

There were times when the tree would not fall after the first three cuts were made. This is where the plastic wedges and ax came into play. It's called "wedging." Uncle Tom put the thin end of the wedge into the back cut and drove it in with his ax. Sometimes, due to the size of the tree, he needed two or three wedges to make the tree fall. Three times that day, Uncle Tom allowed me to drive the wedge in to finish it off. Talk about exciting! I felt like I was a man being out there with him on the job.

After each tree went down, he climbed up on it and bucked it. He then took out his tape to measure the tree's length and diameter at the base. He used a pencil he carried in his shirt pocket to write this information on his aluminum hard hat. At 11:00 a.m., we stopped for lunch. Sitting on a big rock, in the warm sun on the side of a mountain, looking down into a gorgeous valley, made my bologna and cheese sandwich the best one of my life. A half-hour later we got back to work and quit for the day at 2:30. We hauled his gear back to the landing. Uncle Tom sat in his truck and figured out from the entries on his hard hat how many board feet he had felled that day, filled out a report card and gave it to the foreman. I asked him how many trees we cut down and how much money we had made that day. He said he/we felled twenty trees and had earned several hundred dollars. I was amazed someone could make that much money in a single day.

My family stayed in Happy Camp for about ten days on that vacation and had a lot of fun, but for me it was the best because I had spent one of those days in the woods with my Uncle Tom.

My dad was not the only one of his eight brothers who was a fighter. Several of them ended up in scads of barroom scrapes, wherever there was a fight to be found. Every year for many years beginning in the 1960's there was a big family reunion held at Hagaman Park near Stevinson, California on the Merced River. It happened on the Sunday before Memorial Day. My Great Uncle Claude Faddis was the person who kept this going year after year. Uncle Claude was my Grandpa Leonard's brother. Nearly two hundred people whose primary family names were McGowen or Faddis came to these reunions. Uncle Claude arrived at the park on those Sundays by 5:00 a.m. to reserve the large picnic area and tables our family required. He would bring a broom and sweep off the tables under the huge oak trees and tidy up as he waited for everyone to get there. Around 9:00 a.m., folks would begin to arrive and socialize. There was always a guitar or three and those were played and people sang. When I was about seventeen, I began to accompany Uncle Claude on those annual Sunday mornings and we had some wonderful visits. Later, after he passed away, I was the one who took over the responsibility of reserving our spot on Memorial Day Sundays. I was proud to step into Uncle Claude's shoes in this small way.

One year, two of the early arrivers were my Uncle Jim Faddis who lived near the park and our cousin Dennis Faddis from Arizona. Dennis was an ironworker and a very tough man. As the two of them waited for others to arrive, they walked down by the river to talk and drink their beers. While they sat on the riverbank, they saw three young children floating by, obviously unable to swim and in great distress. The men jumped into the water and swam out to the children where Uncle Jim was able to grab two of them and Dennis got one. They made it back to shore safely. The parents of the kids were nowhere in sight so the men walked the youngsters upstream to find their father and some of his friends sitting in lounge chairs. The dad was completely oblivious to what had happened and it was clear he had not been paying attention to his three children wandering off. This made Cousin Dennis very angry, and the father's nonchalance about what had just occurred made Dennis even madder. He told the dad he wanted to talk to him and they walked down by the river where the kids couldn't see them. At that time, Dennis pushed, shoved and slapped the guy around, berating him for what a lousy parent he was.

Another story comes to mind, which illustrates the meanness that can come out of being drunk. It involved my uncle Bill who was the youngest of my father's siblings. In 1981, after my brother Kevin was killed in a car crash, Uncle Bill, Uncle Dick and my grandmother came down from Redding that evening. By then, my mother had spent the entire day in her bedroom mourning her loss. She had told me she did not want to be bothered and the only people she wanted to talk to were her best friend Marion Smith and me. When Grandma and my uncles got there they wanted to see her but I told them she did not wish to speak to anyone at that time. My recollection is that they had all been drinking, and Uncle Bill was especially intoxicated. They tried to pressure me into letting them go into my mom's room, but I was protecting her and her wishes and stood my ground. A little while later as I sat in the living room staring at the TV that had a baseball game on it, Uncle Bill came up to me and said, "If my brother had died today, I wouldn't be sitting here watching TV." I reminded him that when my father, his brother, passed away in 1968, Bill and some other brothers showed up at our house and they were all drunk. And so I told him, "Well, at least I'm not drunk!"

He left the room and walked outside. About ten minutes later, my brother Jeff came to me and told me, "Stan, Uncle Bill wants you to come outside because he wants to fight you." Admittedly, I feared my uncles because they had so much more experience fighting than I did, were tough, and they would not quit. Jeff told me he thought I could beat Uncle Bill because he was drunk. Jeff also had another piece of advice for me. He said, "Stan, if you do fight him, you're going to have to really hurt him or he won't stop because he likes pain." I asked Jeff what he meant by this and he said, "At the very least, you're going to have to break one of his arms." Fortunately, my uncles and my grandmother got in their car and drove to a bar and I didn't see them until the next day when Uncle Bill was sober. He never brought up the incident from the night before and I was relieved that I did not have to fight him.

My maternal grandfather was a rough and simple man. His name was Bert Lee Taylor; he was born on January 26, 1909 in Dallas County, Missouri and passed away on March 30, 1978 at age sixty-nine. He married my grandma, Mildred Cleo Bailey in 1930 when she was sixteen and he was twenty-one. They were the parents of my Aunt Joan, my mom Delores, my Uncle Phil and my Aunt Sue. They were married a total of forty-eight years. I have some great memories of my Grandpa, which I want to share with you.

Grandpa was not a religious man and this fact was painful for my grandmother who had been a Christian since she was a young girl. He was sometimes gruff and wanted things to go his way most of the time, so he could be impatient. But he was also gentle and I remember how he grinned and cackled when something amused him. I've been told he made it as far as the second grade in school. I can imagine he began working early in his life and required no more education to make it through. He worked in Texas building oil rigs for the rich oilmen of that time. Later, after he came to California, he was a carpenter and a "pile driver," working a crew that built bridges and overpasses. At the time he retired he was a foreman for a construction company that built the California Aqueduct canal.

Grandpa liked his beer and I remember several times riding in his old pick-up with him to the store or on a hunting trip. He often had a tall can of Falstaff inside a paper sack, which he sipped on as he drove. He also smoked Swisher Sweets cigars, the smell of which was very unpleasant to me. He wore the same thing every day--a long-sleeved, button-up khaki shirt and khaki pants. Grandpa was what we, these days, call a "road rager," yelling at slowpoke drivers and cussing those who did not navigate the roads like he wanted them to. I was about seven years old when I first saw him flip the bird to another motorist. Grandpa then sternly advised me not make that sign to others, but it wasn't the last time I saw him flip off someone.

Many times after our dad died in 1968, my Grandpa would come to our house and he always brought us a box of groceries. These boxes contained staples such as milk, eggs, bread, bologna, cheese, and bacon made from the jowls of the hog. The box also usually contained treats like Tootsie Rolls, Abba Zabbas or Chick-O-Sticks for his four grandkids. To this day, I don't know why he brought the groceries in a cardboard box instead of paper grocery bags, but it is one of my fondest memories of him.

From 1968 on, my brothers Jeff, Kevin and I went deer and squirrel hunting with Grandpa in the Sierras. We would load up his truck and go camping for several days on the weekends. Several cousins and friends met us there and we had so much fun. Grandpa did the cooking on his old Coleman stove, frying up a big iron skillet full of potatoes, onions and linguica. We also ate bologna sandwiches, beans or Vienna sausages and saltine crackers.

Our hunting routine was that we'd get up at dawn, eat a quick breakfast and go hiking through the woods looking for deer. Each of us would take a different trail or walk the logging roads. Around lunch we headed back to camp where Grandpa was waiting. He'd give us a bologna sandwich or a can of pork and beans to eat. Then Grandpa would announce, "It's time to go hunt some squirrels!" We hunted deer in the morning and evening when they were moving to and from their watering places. In the afternoon, the deer were bedded down but the bushy-tailed gray squirrels were very active gathering pine cone seeds for the winter. Grandpa loved to eat squirrels, which my Grandma prepared chicken-fried for him when we got home.

The squirrel-hunting portion of the day was the most exciting as well as the most terrifying part of our hunts. Grandpa's method was what you would call unorthodox and unlawful. We three boys took turns, alternating with two of us in the back of the truck and the third one riding up front with Grandpa.

The two in the back stood in the truck bed resting our shotguns on the top of the cab. One would cover the right side of the road and the other, the left side. As Grandpa drove slowly along the bumpy logging truck roads, we shotgunners scanned the roadside for the squirrels. If one of us spotted one, we'd holler for him to stop and he'd slam on the brakes. Most often, we took a shot while still standing in the truck. We had to shoot quickly or the squirrel, which was not about to wait around, would escape its fate. Woe to the boy who missed because Grandpa would get mad and yell that we were wasting his shotgun shells.

When Grandpa slammed on the brakes, the shooters in the back of the truck were prepared because it had been one of us who yelled for him to stop, and the centrifugal force pushed us forward against the cab of the truck. The terrifying times were when Grandpa spotted a gray tail on the road in front of him. Without warning, he gassed the truck, quickly speeding up to get to where he saw the squirrel, and we had to hang on for dear life. More than once we fell down or nearly tumbled out of the truck bed. It was simultaneously frightening and fun, especially in light of the fact that as we approached the squirrel Grandpa would often yell, "Shoot! Shoot that son-of-a-b****!" We have laughed about this many times throughout the years. I feel relieved that no one ever got shot or hurt.

I moved away from my hometown in 1976 to escape the life of partying and the bad influences there. At that time I had a good job as a shipping and receiving clerk at WESCO, a division of the Westinghouse Corporation. When I told Grandpa I was quitting WESCO to move to San Jose to go to Bible College, he was upset. He sternly told me I was making a big mistake to quit a good job and wondered what good it would do me to go to Bible College. To him, it was a poor decision. It hurt that he didn't support me and I almost stayed in Ceres because I didn't want him to be angry with me. However, I followed my heart and moved.

In 1977, Grandpa was told he had emphysema and that his time on Earth was short. While he was in the hospital, a preacher who was about my grandfather's age visited him. Grandpa, after all his years of drinking and avoiding God, prayed for salvation and became a Christian. He lived another year and then went home to be with the Lord.

Sometime later, I was talking to Grandma about him. She told me she had loved him very much but admitted that their many years of marriage were hard because of his drinking and short temper. He was in many ways a good husband to her because he provided for the family and protected them. She lamented that for all those years she prayed that Grandpa would someday become a Christian because this would have helped him be a better father and husband and easier to live with. She then told me something I will never forget. She said, "That last year of Bert's life, after he accepted Christ, he was a different man, and that one year made up for all the years of heartache that came before it." I am so looking forward to the day when I'll see them again in heaven.

There were four kids in our family. I am the oldest, Jeff was second, Tina, the third and Kevin the youngest. We also had at least two other siblings, our half-sisters, Dawn and Darla, who were much older than we were and whom I only remember seeing once or twice. Our Dad was their father; he had been married to their mother, Barbara. In fact, Dad was still legally married to Barbara until right before he died in 1968. So he was with my mother all those years while still legally married to Barbara. He finally divorced her and married Mom so that when he passed away, Mom would be entitled to his Social Security and Veteran's pension, not Barbara. I've also heard from a couple of my uncles that Dad also fathered other children while he was with Mom, something I do not doubt, but I have never met any of them.

Most people called my brother Jeff "Jethro Bodeen" or just Bodeen, and it fit him well. His true initials were JB (as in Jeffrey Bert) but a second-grade classmate who was not fond of

Jeff gave him the nickname. The TV show *The Beverly Hillbillies* was popular at that time and the kid thought it was funny to dub him Jethro Bodeen because of his manner of talking, his "redneck" behavior, and that he appeared to not possess a lot of "book learnin'." The nickname stuck with him the rest of his life until his untimely demise at age forty-six. In school, Jeff was enrolled in an EH (educationally handicapped) class. He was hyperactive and epileptic, for which he was prescribed Phenobarbital. Jeff could not sit still and other kids teased him about his behavior. His response was to fight, and many a boy was the target of his wrath. Jeff was tough, unafraid and ferocious when he got mad.

Most people loved Jeff but some strongly disliked him. He was good-looking, rowdy and charismatic. Many guys were jealous of his ability to attract girls. Of course, Jeff had his faults; he was quick to anger and would fight at the drop of a hat. He was self-centered and always wanted to be doing something wild. I used to say that he was born a hundred years too late and would have been a great mountain man or an outlaw. He loved to hunt bear, wild pigs, game birds and raccoons. His method of hunting hogs was unorthodox. While most would shoot a three-hundred-pound hog from a safe distance, Jeff had "catch dogs" that would chase down their prey and latch on to the pig. They held the animal until Jeff got there to stab it with his knife until it died.

When I was twelve and Jeff was eleven, we went one night to a Christian Brigade (aka Royal Rangers, and is much like the Boy Scouts of America) meeting at the First Baptist Church of Ceres. The first (and only) evening of our Royal Ranger careers lasted a total of thirty minutes. About twenty minutes in, Jeff came running to tell me that two other boys were picking on him, challenging him to fight. Since we were raised to protect one another, we went looking for them. Come to find out, they were brothers who went to a different elementary school than us so we didn't know them and they didn't realize who they were messing with. Jeff and I invited the brothers to settle our grievances and they, being confident in their own fighting skills, accepted. We all went outside where Jeff and I beat them up. A couple of leaders intervened, one of whom was the father of the two boys. They sent Jeff and me home, telling us to not come back--ever.

Jeff was really not a troublemaker as much as he was a "trouble magnet." Yes, he had a smart mouth and was fearless. I think his small stature (in high school he was about 5'4" and ninety-five pounds) caused him to be picked on by bigger boys. However, any particular bully only did it once to Bodeen and subsequently received a beating for his trouble. I saw him fight many times and never saw him lose. He refused to surrender.

In those days, Ceres was a farming town and most men wore baseball caps emblazoned with logos such as John Deere and Stanislaus Farm Supply. Jeff had this little trick he used many times in fights, most of which were begun with the combatants arguing, insulting and pushing one another. Jeff would adjust his cap several times by briefly removing it, smoothing back his hair with the other hand and putting the cap back on. His opponent would become accustomed to him doing this during the pre-fight woofing. On the third or fourth hat adjustment, Jeff, instead of putting it back on his head, would grab it by the bill and flip it up in the air a few feet. Every time I saw him do this, the other guy looked up at the airborne hat and Jeff would then punch him in the face. Fight over.

Jeff was also a hunter, trapper and fisherman. He hunted most local game animals including waterfowl, deer, bear, raccoons and wild hogs. He owned many hunting dogs over the years such as Black and Tans, Redbones, Pit Bulls and Weimaraners. He lost a couple of his dogs while hunting coons. On two separate occasions his dogs chased a coon that swam out into the middle of a river, turned and waited for the dog to get to it. The coon then climbed atop the dog's head and held it under the water until it drowned. Raccoons are very smart animals; dogs, not so much.

Another story I heard from our little brother Kevin amazes, but does not surprise me. Jeff and Kevin, along with their friend Kelly Adcock, were hunting bear during bow season. Jeff's dogs treed a big black bear and Jeff shot the bear with several arrows in an effort to kill it so it would fall out of the tree. (My apologies to the anti-hunting contingent, but I'm just the messenger). The bear would not die or come out of the tree all night long. Jeff was out of arrows, so, the next morning, he told Kelly and Kevin to stay there with the dogs while he went to town to buy more arrows. He was unable to procure any so he drove back to the tree at which time the bear (later found to be over 350 pounds) began to climb down to the ground. Not willing to let the wounded bear get away, Jeff found a six-foot tree branch about the size of a man's wrist. Using some duct tape he had in his truck, he lashed his hunting knife to the stick, then used his homemade spear to go after the bear. Kevin and Kelly hid behind some trees and watched Jeff fight the bear as they alternately chased each other. Several times the bear stood on its back legs and fought Jeff and his dogs who were circling the bear, trying to bite it as they were trained to do. The bear finally succumbed and another story to tell around the campfire was born--Bodeen and the Bear.

Jeff often asked if he could take my son, Daniel, hunting with him to which I always said no. Jeff was a poacher, an outlaw, and he hunted at night and on private property without the owner's permission. There was no way I was going to allow my boy to go with Bodeen anywhere. Over the years Jeff acquired a large key ring full of keys that opened the many gates to the properties he wished to hunt. These keys were bought, sold, copied and stolen. Ranchers, the Pacific Gas and Electric Company, and Gallo owned most of these properties. More than once he was chased by ranchers and game wardens that tried to catch him doing something illegal, which he did constantly. Those in pursuit also had keys to the gates, so, when he saw a vehicle coming from afar, he sped off, going through, opening and closing locked gates as he went. Usually, he could make it to a main road or canal bank well ahead of his pursuers and make a clean get away. When he thought they were getting too close, he would take a lock sitting on his truck seat and for which those making chase did not have a key, and lock the gate with it. Chase over.

One last story . . . during the salmon run in the Tuolumne River between Waterford and LaGrange, CA, Bodeen practiced the art of "snagging." It's done by attaching a very large and heavy treble hook to a fishing pole line and casting it out into the river, then reeling it in an attempt to snag the fish. This was done under the cover of darkness and is highly illegal (what a surprise, huh?). One night, Jeff and our cousin, Larry Sabo, who was enrolled in high school at the time, snagged dozens of salmon ranging in size from ten to twenty-eight pounds. Half of Jeff's small pickup bed was full of fish when they left the next morning. Larry was late for school and was worried the teacher wouldn't let him into the classroom. This was not a problem for Bodeen. He drove across campus to a set of portable classrooms where Larry was supposed to have been ten or fifteen minutes earlier. Jeff went into the classroom and asked the male teacher to come outside so he could talk to him about Larry's tardiness. Jeff took responsibility for the situation, explaining they had "fished" all night long and miscalculated how long it would take to get back in time. He pointed out the truck bed full of fish and told the teacher to pick out any two salmon he wanted in order to make amends. Without a word the man grabbed two fish and told Larry his tardiness was forgiven. The problem was solved.

Jeff was fifteen months younger than me and as children we were very close. We had little contact after 1976 when I moved to San Jose. We did not see eye-to-eye on most things in life and we argued a lot when we were together. In 2005, Jeff wrecked his truck, was ejected and badly injured. He had been drinking at a pizza parlor just prior to the crash. Jeff was comatose for two weeks in the ICU at Doctor's Hospital before dying on February 8, 2005, after suffering a stroke.

For many years, I believed my brother was mentally ill because he could become quickly violent and vicious when provoked in the slightest way. If he believed he was being wronged he reacted instantly and with rage. I later found that Jeff's uncontrolled anger was due to the fact he abused alcohol and used methamphetamine. Toward the end of his life, he was drinking as much as a fifth of whiskey a day. After I learned about all this, Jeff confided in me that he was once one of the biggest meth dealers in the county and often had as much as $45,000 buried in his backyard. When he became worried the police were going to catch him, he stopped selling it.

The story that best illustrates Jeff's instability is when he worked for a company that manufactured metal boxes used in buildings to house electrical components such as light switches and outlets. Jeff was one of the workers who spot-welded these things together and he was very quick. While his coworkers averaged welding 175 per day, Jeff would do 300+. He loudly whistled and sang country western songs while he worked and it was annoying to those around him. Of course he couldn't have cared less about what others thought.

He got carpal tunnel syndrome in both wrists due to the repetitiveness of the welding, and the company doctor took him off work so he could have surgery. Upon his recovery, the doctor released him to go back, but when he reported for work, he was told he no longer had a job because he had been off too long. Jeff immediately hired a Worker's Comp attorney who had him back on the job the next day. Although Jeff was a productive employee, his loud behavior annoyed enough people who complained so the company tried to get rid of him. Prior to going off work on disability, Jeff had been assigned to the swing shift, working from 3 p.m. to 11 p.m. Almost every night after work he headed out with his dogs to hunt all night and then return to work on time the next day. He could function on little or no sleep thanks to the methamphetamine.

Knowing that he liked working "swings" the boss moved him to the 7 a.m. to 3 p.m. shift to try and make him quit. This angered Jeff a lot and so he began to threaten several of the men in charge, telling them that if they didn't stop messing with him, he would kill them. This was reported to the local police who told the supervisors that there was nothing that could be done about the verbal threats. Upon learning this, Jeff kept it up. For the first time in their history, the company hired a security company to be on duty when Jeff was working. Finally, the administration asked Jeff what it would take to make him go away. He told them he would quit if they gave him $10,000 and kept his dental insurance effective for one year so that he could have his own teeth and those of his two sons fixed. They agreed and Jeff left the company. The following week he called the dentist to make an appointment and was told the company cancelled his coverage the previous day. Jeff drove to the job site and threatened bodily harm and death to six administrators. He told at least one of them he wouldn't kill him quickly, but would catch him out on the dark road the man lived on and slowly skin him with sharp knives until the man begged Jeff to kill him.

Jeff got out of there before the police showed up, went home and called me to say goodbye. He said, "I'm going to kill every one of those sons of bitches and I won't be taken alive. I'm gonna shoot it out with the cops until they kill me." I immediately called his former boss and told him he was in grave danger because I was certain Jeff was capable of doing such a heinous thing. I also told him they should not have reneged on their agreement to keep Jeff's dental insurance active. To this day, I cannot believe his reply. He said, "Mister Faddis, we do not appreciate you calling to threaten us like this." I said, "I am not threatening you, I am warning you that you might die tonight if you don't try to make things right with him." I explained I was a probation officer and had a duty to warn someone I thought was in danger from someone else. He told me they would think about it and asked for my callback number.

The following day, they called me and offered to pay Jeff $7,000 more to cover the work the dentist said it would take to do the dental work. They further advised they did not want to see or talk to Jeff and would only work with me to wrap up the situation. So, a couple of days later, I drove from San Jose to Modesto, picked up Jeff and dropped him at a nearby park while I went to the company office. I was given a typed agreement for him to sign in which he would promise to not come within five-hundred yards of the job site or any employee, agree that the $7,000 sum would fully satisfy his grievances, and that he would not have any contact at all with anyone associated with the company. Additionally, he had to agree not to damage any property of the company or its employees and not threaten, harm, maim or kill any employee of the company. I took the document to Jeff at the park for him to sign and returned it to the office. I was handed a check for the agreed-upon amount and took it to my brother. He looked at it and said he couldn't cash it because he didn't have a bank account. I went back to the office and explained to them. They called their bank to say Jeff would be coming there soon to cash the check and to let him do it. I waited for him and watched as he walked out of the bank. He was smiling as he stuffed $7,000 worth of hundreds, fifties, twenties, and tens in the pockets of his cutoff jeans. Not one cent of that money ever made to the dentist's office and no one's teeth ever got fixed.

My little sister, Tina Gay Faddis, was third in line and the only girl in our family. She was a tad more than three years younger than me, and was between Jeff and Kevin in birth order. Tina was born August 3, 1960 and had the same birthday as my daughter, Heather, who was born exactly twenty-five years later.

I remember Tina being a happy young girl. She was very smart, pretty and she liked to play with the other kids in our neighborhood. We lived on a cul-de-sac that had six houses and a duplex, and each one had several kids living in them. The busiest house was across the street from us where the six Hair kids lived. Many days were spent having fun outside with all those kids. We played softball and hide-and-seek and wrestled on the lawn.

Being the only girl in our family, Tina was teased a lot by the three of us boys. We made her laugh with our joking and she would get all worked up to the point she had to pee. Several times she was not able to make it to the bathroom in time which made us laugh all the more. One benefit of having brothers was their protection. None of the punks at school gave her a hard time because they all knew she was Stan and Jeff Faddis's little sister. Tina was eight when our father died and I think she appreciated that her brothers watched out for her.

One day when she was about ten, on her way home from school, she walked by a house that had a sign on the fence that said, "Free Kittens." She asked our mom if she could have one of them. Mom consented and so Tina started to leave to walk back down to the house to get it. I had a gut feeling that the old man who lived there was a pervert so I decided to tag along.

At that time, I had a coat that looked like it was made from a grizzly bear hide. If you have ever seen the TV show *Third Rock from the Sun*, one of the characters wears a coat exactly like it. It had long brown and black fur and a hood. The lining was bright orange nylon material. I had the coat on the day we walked to the man's house. We went to the back door that led to the laundry room where the kittens were kept in a cardboard box. I stood to the side so the old man could not see me when he opened the door. The man answered the knock and Tina told him she had come to get a kitten. Thinking that she was alone, the man said she could have a kitty but she had to kiss him to get it. He beckoned her to come into the laundry room. My blood boiled as I realized my suspicions were true. I stepped into the doorway so he could see me and advised him that I would kill him if he touched my little sister. My thirteen-

year-old heart was beating hard as I said this and I was scared
beyond belief. I told Tina to pick a kitten out of the box sitting
by the washing machine, which she did, and we beat it out of
there. Later, we were able to laugh about it and wondered if the
old pervert thought a grizzly bear was about to get him when
he first saw me. From then on, when I walked by his house, if
he was in the yard or on his porch, I'd glare at him and he
would silently go back into his house.

The two things I could not protect my little sister from
were the poor choices she made about men and about drugs.
One of her boyfriends got her started using illegal substances.
My recollection is that she first started by using inhalants, also
known as "huffing." This is done by spraying aerosol paint into
a plastic bag and inhaling the fumes. Since I was away at college
when this all started, I was unable to take steps prevent it;
however, I believe that even if I had been there I could not
have stopped her. Jeff was there but I don't know if he tried to
stop her because, as I did not learn until much later, Jeff was
also using drugs.

One summer, when I was home from college, Tina
called the house to say she needed help. Some guy had taken
her (she went willingly) to Coalinga where they were staying in
a motel. He was a truck driver and was hauling tomatoes to the
canneries around there. After a couple of weeks she wanted to
leave, but he refused to take her home. I drove the hundred
miles south to the cheap, rundown motel they were staying in.
He was surprised to see me because Tina did not tell him I was
coming. He said he wasn't going to let her leave. I told him he
could let her go without incident or he could have me stomp a
mud hole in him. I said either way didn't matter, but my sister
was going to come with me. He did not protest any further and
so we left.

At some point in her use of drugs, Tina began using heroin intravenously. She once told me her habit was so severe that she could easily shoot six hundred dollars of heroin a day, if she had it. You can imagine the terrible things she did in order to support her drug abuse. One way was to commit burglaries looking for cash and things she could sell on the street. In the early 80's she was convicted of six first-degree burglaries and sent to State Prison for eight years. After her release, she violated her parole many times and went back and forth from freedom to custody.

Our mother and I tried many times to get Tina to seek help for her drug abuse, but the only person not interested in treatment was her. The sadness of this is beyond comprehension. On June 23, 2005, at age forty-four, Tina was driving herself and her boyfriend to the Chicken Ranch Casino in Jamestown, California. She was flying high on methamphetamine. Driving down a sloping curve near a bluff called Lover's Leap, her vehicle crossed the center line and hit an oncoming car head-on. The crash killed Tina as well as the woman driving the other vehicle and severely injured one of that lady's two children. Tina's boyfriend was unscathed.

Our youngest brother, Kevin Dean Faddis, was born on October 22, 1962. He was six at the time our father passed away. Kevin was the light of our little family. He was funny, outgoing, and looked like Dad. I don't really remember exactly when he began to stray away from our mom's teaching against drugs and alcohol, but it was probably when he was a freshman in high school. He started hanging around with a rough crowd, and began using tobacco, alcohol and marijuana.

Shortly after getting his driver's license, he got into trouble for spinning donuts on the grass of the new Smyrna

Park in Ceres and ended up in Juvenile Hall. In court, he was ordered to pay a fine and perform some community service work. I was not privy to the details of this incident or other run-ins he may have had with law enforcement because I was away at college by then and Mom didn't want to worry me.

In 1979, Kevin was riding in the back of a pickup that had five of his friends in it. They were coming back from a hunting trip in the Sierras. The driver wrecked the truck by going over a 300-foot embankment. Kevin was thrown clear and landed face down on a pile of rocks. He was taken to Doctor's Hospital in Modesto where it was found he had a brain injury. He was comatose, and the doctors couldn't guarantee that he would ever wake up.

At the time this happened, I had just finished the season working in the cannery, so it was decided I would spend as much time as possible with him in the hospital. Dr. John Darroch, his neurosurgeon, told me I should speak to Kevin as if he were awake. So, I talked to him a lot about what was going on at home, with his friends, and about memories of our times together. I even talked to him about what was playing on the TV in his room, which was mostly talk shows, game shows and soap operas.

One day, I began to wonder if he could actually hear me. His right hand was resting on his chest and I tapped his forefinger and told him, "Kevin, if you can hear me, lift up this finger." And he did! I told him to answer me by raising one finger for "yes" and two fingers for "no." He did so as I asked him if he knew where he was (yes), if he remembered what happened (no), and if he could open his eyes (no). This method of communication only worked intermittently and the doctor said it was probably related to the swelling and ebbing of his brain. But, the fact he could hear us gave great hope that he might someday regain consciousness.

Three weeks after being admitted to the hospital, I was spending the day with him. As usual, I was chatting to him about something on the TV. I glanced at him just in time to see his eyes flutter open. He looked at me and said, "I want some ice cream." I said, "You can have all the ice cream you want, buddy!" I hollered for the nurse who came rushing in, probably thinking something was wrong. She was astonished to see Kevin looking at her with fully opened eyes.

Little Dog was in the hospital a total of 39 days. When he went home, he could not return to school immediately and needed twenty-four-hour care for the first thirty days, so I volunteered. Our Mom needed to continue working to keep the insurance active. Kevin was very popular in high school, so every day I drove him up and down Whitmore Avenue (the cruise) twice a day, at noon and after school. He was able to stay in touch with his friends this way and they appreciated what I was doing for him. I was five or more years older than these kids and at first I felt like an intruder into my little brother's life. But they all liked me and thought I was cool. I even took him to some parties and to the Ceres Drive-In to hang out with his buddies.

The memories of this time in our lives thirty-five years ago are precious to me. However, Kevin's stay on earth ended on August 15, 1981, when he crashed his Toyota four-wheel drive truck in a single car wreck and died. His friend Kelly Adcock was also in the truck but he was uninjured.

Kevin either fell asleep because he was tired or, as the doctors speculated, he may have blacked out. He reportedly had suffered several blackouts following his brain injury in 1979. One of these occurred when he was driving a tractor in an orchard and ran into a tree. The autopsy showed he was under the influence of several illegal drugs including cocaine and marijuana as well as alcohol. He was the first of my siblings to suffer severe consequences as a result of making poor choices.

Over four hundred people attended his memorial service. This was a great tribute to what a good kid he was and I was blessed to have had him for my little brother. Both my brothers are dead now because they made the same bad choice- - they drove drunk. Kevin died instantly as a result of his single-car crash. Jeff lasted for two weeks after his single car wreck, dying of a stroke in the intensive care unit. I thank God that their actions did not kill or injure anyone else.

Here is something I wrote about Kevin in 2006:

Twenty-five years ago today, on August 15, 1981, my youngest brother, Kevin Dean Faddis, died in a car crash. He was eighteen years old. He would now be forty-three and I often wonder what kind of a man that kid would have grown to be had he survived the crash. Not surprisingly, I am in a funk today as I remember that tragic day long ago. I am writing this to help me deal with the blue mood I'm in.

"Little Dog" as I called him was a funny, sometimes rowdy, often gentle young man. He called me "Big Dog." The two of us, along with our middle brother, Jeff, (aka: Jethro Bodeen) did a lot of things together when we were kids. Bodeen has also died (February 2005 at age forty-six) and thinking about the loss of both my little brothers is hurting me a lot right now.

I sometimes ask myself, "Would Kevin and Jeff have made the decision to drive drunk if they fully understood how much emotional pain they have caused to those who love them?" The ones they left behind. The loss of my brothers at such early ages has hurt me beyond belief. We can no longer hunt, fish, and laugh together. It is because of those bad choices that I sometimes become angry with my little brothers. It was a stupid thing for them to do. I still love them and treasure the memories, but they have hurt me a lot by this. I find it interesting that I asked the same questions about my son's demise as I did regarding my brothers' deaths. That is . . . had they pondered the ramifications of their choices prior to driving drunk or pulling the trigger, would they still have done it?

When I think back on the family I came from, and my upbringing, I sometimes wonder what things would have been like if my dad had not gotten paralyzed and had lived a lot longer. I think in a lot of ways we had a good life but I also realize now that my dad would probably have continued to be a philanderer and an alcoholic and I don't know how that would have turned out. Probably not well. I think my mom would have stayed with him but it may not have improved beyond what they had lived up to the time it all ended.

Where my siblings were concerned, my mother was often not able to keep them from making disastrous choices. My sister Tina felt she needed to have attention from males because she wanted to be loved. Unfortunately, the guys she was attracted to were the type no man would want his daughter to be with. Mom just wasn't strong enough to tell these guys to go away. When I think of Kevin, I realize that, after his car crash in 1979, he had a brain injury that caused him to have blackouts and his judgment was impaired. He didn't have a lot of parameters for behavior. This caused him to hang out with people who were on the seedy side of life. His personality was just as good as Jeff's and our dad's. People loved being with him because he was funny and friendly; he was magnetic. As for Jeff, I learned before he died that not only did he naturally have a bad temper that caused him to get into numerous fights and other destructive situations, but he had been using methamphetamine for twenty-five years, which messed him up even worse.

In many ways I wanted to be like my dad. I wanted to be tough, popular like he was and financially successful because I did consider my dad to be a successful man in his work in construction. But of course he died before I could figure these things out. So when my father died, followed by my maternal grandfather's death a year later, I had no father figure to look up to except my uncles. As I have already said, they were not men I wanted to emulate because I didn't want to be like them. I wanted to be my own person. I was so fortunate that God had different plans for me and I know He called me. It took me a long time to see the big picture and become fully committed to Him; I believe I am finally on the right track. Of course, I still have room to grow; however, I am now able see the importance of putting God first in my life because that causes everything else to fall into place.

When I think about not being the same person I was, I know that if I had continued to follow the path my family set for me, I probably would not have met and married Linda, and even if I had we probably would not still be married. I don't think I would have been as successful as I've been because God led me through my education and into my career. Had I not met the Lord, I don't know what I would have become. My wife and children are gifts that have come to me out of my relationship with God. Many of the best things in my life have come out of how I have learned over time to honor the Lord. I certainly didn't, and still don't, deserve all the grace I have been given. I believe had I not met Jesus I would be just like so many of those in my family who have suffered from their own bad choices.

It is because of Christ that I chose to go down a different road, and ended up not having the same problems as my siblings. I am forever grateful that God had his hand on me. As I write about this, I become overwhelmed again at how much God has blessed me. Even though I know I don't have to thank Him for loving me, I still am amazed that He loves me as an individual. I am not the same person I was and not the same person I would have been if it weren't for the changes God has made in my life.

Chapter Two

While my upbringing was certainly not perfect, my childhood was good in many ways because the four of us kids had a mother that deeply loved us. However, she did not really have the tools she needed to raise us to be more disciplined and healthy. As a parent now I understand she was tired and didn't really know best how to raise us. She wanted us to be happy, and sometimes that meant she was not tough enough on us. (Although she wasn't against using the belt when we needed it!) I remember one time my brother Jeff and I got into a fistfight and he punched me in the nose and made it bleed. I was lying there on the carpet in the living room trying to stop the bleeding when my mother came in. Instead of being concerned with my injury, she had the belt with her. She was angry that I might bleed on the carpet. Although that wasn't pleasant at the time, I know now how hard it must have been for her to try to contain four rowdy kids.

Most of our adventures centered on hunting and fishing. Our mom often drove us down to the Tuolumne River and dropped us off to fish and would pick us up at dark to haul us home. We earned money by harvesting freshwater clams from a huge clam bed our dad had shown us on the river. We sold the clams to a local bait store. Mom also took us to our favorite dove and pheasant hunting spots, to the roller-skating rink and the movies whenever she could afford to so.

One of my favorite stories about my two brothers Jeff and Kevin and me is about a particular fishing trip. We fished together quite a bit, all over several counties in our area including Stanislaus, Merced, Tuolumne and San Joaquin. Usually, we took an old green metal Coleman ice chest on our expeditions in which we put our lunch and soda pop. Later in the day we put our catch of fish or the bullfrogs we had gigged in it.

One day we fished the Merced River, downstream from Lake McSwain, east of Snelling, CA. An elderly woman owned the property on the Merced where we liked to fish. She had given our dad permission to fish there many years before and then also let us have access. The river there had a dam that was designed to allow the water to run over its top, slowing down the flow into shallows in which we could wade and fish. The Merced hosts, among others, trout, salmon, bass, crappie, perch, carp, California pike, bluegill and catfish.

At the time of this story, which occurred in 1974, I was seventeen, Jeff was sixteen, and Kevin was twelve. We were fishing about thirty yards apart in water up to our knees, casting into the deeper water in the middle of the river. Jeff was the furthest upstream, Kevin was in between us and I was downstream. We were all catching fish and releasing the smallest ones. The fish we kept we either ate or gave them to friends and family.

It was salmon spawning season and we saw several big females swimming upstream, sometimes going right by us within a few feet. Suddenly, I heard Jeff yell, "I got a big one! Kevin, help me! I can't hold him!" Kevin was closest to Jeff and he began to run upstream to Jeff, whom I saw was fighting what had to be a huge fish. His rod was bent almost in half and he was hollering, "Hurry! Help me!" I was also moving toward the action and my heart was pounding with the anticipation of seeing how big this fish must be. As Kevin got there, Jeff screamed, "Grab it or it'll get away! Jump on it!" I was about fifteen yards away when Kevin flopped into the water to help his big brother land the fish. He wrapped his arms around it and stood up, and Jeff began to hoot and slap the water. As

Kevin held the fish I saw that it was a dead salmon and its scales and flesh were sliding off its bones.

We then learned Jeff saw the fish floating by him. He grabbed it, hooked his fishing lure into its mouth and pretended he was fighting a huge live salmon. It was big and we estimated it to weigh twenty-five pounds. Kevin was left with rotting fish on his hands and the front of his shirt and pants. We all laughed at the brilliance of Jeff's prank.

After we finished our day of fishing we walked back to Jeff's truck. Kevin's clothes stank like rotten fish, and Jeff didn't want that smell in his pick-up, so he gave Kevin a choice--strip and ride naked in the cab with us, or ride in the truck bed. Kevin enjoyed the fresh air in the back as we drove home that day.

Kevin killed his first and only deer when he was thirteen or fourteen years old. He was walking down an old logging road by himself when he spied a deer standing off the road about fifty feet. The buck was on the other side of a fallen tree, just looking at him. Little Dog made a perfect shot, hitting the deer in the neck. Kevin didn't know what to do after that, so he took off his orange hunting vest, laid it and his gun on the dead deer and ran the three miles all the way back to camp. Two hunters encountered him when his yelling attracted their attention. They told him they would help him get his deer back to camp if he showed them where it was. He refused, accusing them of plotting to rob him of his kill. I heard Kevin yelling while he was still a mile away. "Stan, Grandpa, Jeff, I shot a deer! I shot a deer!" I don't think I ever saw my Grandpa smile as big as he did that day as we hauled that buck into our camp. He was so proud.

Sometimes the three of us fought other boys who were as rowdy as we were. Sometimes we fought each other, but in spite of our feuding, we loved each other like only brothers can. We stood united in all things. When we were together, we were braver than when alone or with our friends, and it felt like nothing could keep us down. We were the sons of Gene Faddis, the toughest son-of-a-gun in Stanislaus County. We knew we were poor country boys and were proud of it. People called us "hillbillies," "trailer trash" and "okies." We didn't care, but when someone called us those names, they had best be farther than an arm's length away and faster than an angry Jethro Bodeen who could run down anyone who needed, as we called it, a "tune-up."

My Dad spanked us whenever he thought it necessary and that put fear into us. He used several belts--a thin dress belt; a thicker and wider, heavier belt; as well as a couple of others, whatever was handy. A story that always makes me smile was the one my mother told many times about the belts. Apparently, they all disappeared, not to be found for a couple of weeks. I guess those two weeks were quiet ones during which my dad did not need to spank us. One day, as Mom was washing dishes, she looked out the window and saw something shiny in our sandbox in the back yard. She went out to see what it was and found four belts bundled up and buried in the sand. My brother Jeff admitted he had put them there because he was tired of getting spanked with them. He received a spanking from our father that evening for his ploy.

My first introduction to church was through a pastor that lived a couple of doors down from us on Camelia Court in Ceres. I was about seven years old when Reverend M.J. Arechuk of the Church of the Nazarene began taking me and a few other neighbor kids to church. Several months later, our family moved to Dale Avenue, one block from the church, so I walked there on Sundays. My parents were not churchgoers.

They neither encouraged nor discouraged me from going and my recollection is that they were neutral on the issue. They slept in in while I got up and went by myself. I do not remember our family observing any type of "Christian" events such as saying grace before meals, celebrating either Easter or Christmas, other than hunting eggs we had colored the day before and getting presents. It was just not part of my parents' raising their kids. We were taught to be respectful of our elders, behave in school, to say "please" and "thank you" when appropriate and to not steal. In short, we were taught to be "good" but God really was not a component of the equation.

I remember my mom commenting several times about what a small child I was. She said I was the littlest kid in my Kindergarten class; even the girls were bigger than me. This all changed in the fifth grade when I began to gain weight and get taller. Since my father died when I was in the fifth grade, I believe that I began to get fat then because I turned to food for solace. Eating made me feel better and so I ate a lot. I have since struggled with a weight problem and have failed to overcome it for forty-five years. The close companion to my fatness is low self-esteem. I didn't think very highly of myself and I was lazy in many ways. I was not a good student and didn't care. I had little confidence in myself and I wanted people to like me so I went out of my way to do nice things for others. One of those things was to cook and serve breakfast in bed to my uncles (Dad's brothers) and their wives or girlfriends when they came to visit. I wanted their approval so much and this is one way I tried to get it. Unfortunately, my uncles considered this a "girly" thing because in their world, cooking was for women to do. Some years later, one of my uncles told me that several of his brothers had decided that I must be a homosexual and that they had resented me for being a "sissy."

62

One thing that has stuck with me for almost fifty years now that I cannot forget occurred when I was ten. My dad, who was sitting in his wheelchair, was changing a flat tire on our station wagon in the driveway. I came out of the house to watch him after I had just washed my hands. He told me to grab hold of the tire and prop it up against the car. I told him I had just washed my hands and didn't want to get them dirty. Dad looked at me with rage in his eyes and said, "You little queer! Do what I tell you!" Being called a name by my father wounded me deeply and to this day I am saddened whenever I recall it. I am sorry to say that being yelled at by my dad on many occasions did not deter me from being a "yeller" with my own children. I didn't call them harsh names like "queer" but I did speak overly loud and harshly to them sometimes. They were so intimidated by me. This is one of my biggest regrets as a father. I love my children deeply, but I have such a quick temper that I often said things in the wrong way. For this I am ashamed.

Senator Robert Francis Kennedy died at 1:44 a.m. on June 6, 1968. I mention it here because this event resulted indirectly in a traumatic event for me later that day. Be patient, as it will take me a minute to get to that. The name of our school's principal is not used out of respect for his anonymity.

I was in Miss Lum's fifth grade class at Whitmore Elementary School in my hometown of Ceres, CA at that time. Some of my classmates included Ron Megee, Debbie Rayford, Dave Stiffler, Eddie Morrow, Rita Woodral, Tim Crownover, Debbie Fabela, Robbie Spears, Jonni Dunnegan, and Mark Lowe.

During lunchtime, the school allowed kids to go home for lunch but we weren't supposed to go anywhere else. Being the adventurous and unbridled boys we were, some of us would go instead to Ceres Billiards to shoot pool and play pinball. On one of these days, not the day mentioned above, a few of us-- Eddie, Dave and Tim--went to the pool hall for our usual routine. The pinball repairman was there working on some of his machines. When it was time to hightail it back to school, we went out the rear door into the alley. One of us noticed the pinball guy's truck parked there with a carton of Camel cigarettes sitting on the dash. Eddie, who smoked on occasion, dared me to grab the carton. Being the tough and unafraid junior thug I was at the time, I reached inside the unlocked truck and grabbed it. We were all very surprised to find no packs of Camels in there. Instead it was full of quarters, dimes and nickels. I do not recall exactly how much money was there, but it was more than thirty dollars. I am ashamed to say we gave no thought to not taking the money. As the one who took the risk of grabbing the loot and having it in my possession at the moment, I decreed that the other three guys could split half of it because I was going to take half for myself. They reluctantly agreed and we divvied up the take.

On the day Bobby Kennedy died, our teacher, Miss Lum, brought a TV into the classroom so we could all watch the news. Everyone was gathered around the set and several of the girls were crying. Not being one for current events and probably not even knowing who Robert Kennedy was, I went into the cloakroom. Whitmore School was built in the early 1900's and each of its classrooms had a separate room where the kids hung up their coats and scarves and left their rain boots. I recollect that Robbie Spears and I were not interested in the TV so we went into the cloakroom to amuse ourselves. We cracked some jokes, shot the breeze and did the "trick" whereby one person "pulls a spider web" from the other's hand. If you're too young to know about this, ask someone over fifty.

At lunchtime, I decided to go to the billiard hall. No one wanted to go along so I rode my bike the two blocks and played some pinball. As I rode back onto the school grounds, I saw what could only be described as an angry mob awaiting my return. There were about a dozen of them and standing in front was Debbi Fabela. She was visibly angry. Her curly black hair and serious overbite contributed to the look of hate on her face. I parked my bike in the rack and walked toward them wondering what was going on. Next thing I know, I was jumped on, knocked down and was being kicked by them with Debbie especially delivering some side busters to my ribs. Finally, some teachers rescued me, but then I was taken to see the school's principal.

Later, I learned why I had been jumped and beaten. While I was gone to Ceres Billiards, Robbie Spears told all the kids in our class that I had been laughing at Debbi Fabela who had been one of the girls crying about Senator Kennedy's passing. This was patently untrue because I am not one to make light of such sadness. If I had laughed about any crying, Debbi Fabela was not one I would have done this toward. She was tough and not a just a little bit intimidating. She was the first girl I can recall using the "f" word. Robbie was a troublemaker who took delight in causing problems. His older brother was rumored to be a gang member who got into fights every weekend in Modesto in the alley behind the Covell Theater. His gang reportedly battled others with knives, chains and broken bottles. Robbie aspired to be just like his big brother and he had a mean streak. On that day, I was a victim of his cruel humor.

To add insult to injury, my journey to Mr. Principal's office was not for the purpose of protecting me. While I was there, I was in trouble for going off campus to an unauthorized location. This came to Mr. Principal's attention as a result of my undeserved beating, which would have been punishment enough. However, he gave me two swats with his spanking paddle for my transgression.

As a postscript I offer this: Miss Lum, a sweet little Chinese woman was well out of her league with her group of fifth grade students that year. It has been a topic of discussion among those of us who have remained in contact since then that the year was Miss Lum's rookie season as a teacher. She meant well and tried hard to teach us what the curriculum called for, but we were adept at getting her to go off topic and discuss other things such as drugs (remember, we were children of the 60's) and English cuss words (we taught them to her).

Apparently, school authorities decided she was not cut out to be a teacher at Whitmore Elementary. This would have been all well and good had it not been for the poor decision about when and how she was informed of her termination. On the last day of school, Miss Lum was summoned to the office at the lunch break and told that her services would no longer be required there. After lunch, a group of fifth graders returned to the classroom to find our beloved Miss Lum sitting at her desk, crying. We were shocked, sad and angered. To this day, I cannot understand why Mr. Principal handled this situation in that manner. It was one of the saddest days of my life up to that point.

After school, several of us (Ron Megee, Tim Crownover, Dave Stiffler and Eddie Morrow) exacted revenge on the principal. Ron Megee may dispute he was one of the evil doers that day and Tim is no longer with us to defend himself, but I strongly believe my recollection is accurate. At any rate, Eddie had one of those "Hi, My Name Is:" name tags that adhere to one's shirtfront. Dave drew a picture on it of a hand flipping the "bird." I believe the "f" word was also written on it to let the principal know the level of our anger. The name tag was placed on the windshield of his VW bus and we threw a dozen or so water balloons into the open windows. I admit that this vengeful act was especially sweet for me because of the swats I had received from the man just the week before.

As many of you have deduced by now, my ramblings here are quite random. This one is no exception and goes back to 1970 or so when I was twelve years old and in school at Walter White Junior High. I have several memories about those two years, one of which involved some fake vomit and a pretty teacher of ours in seventh grade. Her name was Ms. Stapp who all the boys thought was "neat" and "foxy." She was tall, had dark hair and was really nice to everyone. One day, Mark Lowe came to school with a flat rubber mass that looked just like real vomitus.

Mark dared me to play a joke on Ms. Stapp with the fake vomit. So, in the middle of the morning period in her classroom, he asked her for some "help" with his schoolwork. When she walked over to his desk, her back turned to me, I stood up, bent over, made a loud upchucking sound and slapped that faux vomit on the floor. It sounded like something wet hitting the linoleum. Miss Stapp quickly turned toward me, saw that I had just puked and quickly grabbed a wastebasket and brought it over to me. She was so concerned that I was sick and, at that moment, I suddenly wished that I hadn't played this prank. I recall her saying, "Stanley, are you okay?" with great concern. Mark Lowe burst out laughing and I quickly admitted to the prank and picked up the "puke" which caused the boys to roar with laughter; however, the girls were more disgusted about it and sympathetic toward Ms. Stapp. The stunt landed me in the principal's office and from then on, I could not look Ms. Stapp in the eye due to my shame.

In 1995, at the twenty-year reunion of our high school graduation, one of our classmates, whom I will call Joey, told a story to a group of guys standing near the dance floor. I had to admit that I didn't recall the incident until Joey was retelling it twenty-five years later. He said that when we were in the seventh grade, a big eighth grader who was in a special education class approached him. The kid told Joey, who was much smaller; that they were going to go out to the back of the school's field where Joey was going to [perform an oral act] on the bigger kid. Joey panicked and took off running to find me to help him get out of this horrible predicament. He said he found me at my locker. He explained what was happening to which I immediately stated, "Where is he?"

We went searching for the bully and found him in the main hallway. Joey said I walked up to the kid, grabbed him by the front of his shirt and slammed him against the lockers. I then put my face within inches of his and asked, "You see this little guy here?" and gestured toward Joey. The guy nodded and I said, "Well, if you EVER go near him again, I will find you and kill you! Understand?" Joey said the guy was shaking violently as he nodded he did. According to Joey, from that day forward, not only did the kid not speak a word to him, but also if he saw Joey walking down the hallway toward him, he turned and went the other way.

I cannot help but think now of how those of us who were in junior high in 1970-1971 were so naïve. Maybe the kids who lived in Ceres were way behind the curve even at that time, but I don't think so. Today's twelve- and thirteen-year-olds are far more sophisticated and less innocent than we were, in my opinion. The guys I hung around with had no sexual experience and were very vague about how such things worked. We liked girls and wanted to kiss them and maybe even "feel them up" but that is about as far as it went. We liked to socialize with the opposite sex and had fun at school dances and flirting on the playground.

Mark Lowe had some cool parties at his house in high school: however, it was my parties in junior high that everyone anticipated and talked about. My mom was very generous to allow a bunch of pre-teenagers to invade her home, but I think she really enjoyed it. I threw two parties each in the seventh and eighth grades. They were held in our backyard on Kay Street in Ceres. We lived in government housing since we were a "low income" family. Just outside the back door there was a rectangular slab of cement that was roughly twenty by ten feet and the clothesline was strung the length of it. We had a record player that Mom set up for us on the porch and several of the kids who came to the party brought their favorite records. My mother also liked music and owned albums by the Beatles, Herman's Hermits, Simon and Garfunkel and the Byrds. She also had some Johnny Cash, Charley Pride and Willie Nelson, but these guys were not invited to my parties. In order to help make our dancing pleasure more fun, Mom grated some hand soap scraps onto the cement slab so the kids could easily slide our shoes as we danced to the music.

I think the song "Spirit in the Sky" by Norman Greenbaum was the most played record. "Venus" by Shocking Blue, "Green-Eyed Lady" by Sugarloaf, "Ma Belle Amie" by Tee Set and "Tears of a Clown" by Smokey Robinson and the

Miracles were some of the favorites. Of course, "I'll Be There" by the Jackson Five was the best slow dance song up until that time. Chicago's "Color My World" replaced it when we got to high school. The dancing was fun but the highlight of these parties was the "make out" area. It was a dark place around the side of our house where the kids would sneak over to kiss a little bit. As I said before, we were very naive so kissing was as far as it went. Sure, the boys talked about taking it a step further, but as far as I know, no one in our circle of friends did. I have no clue what the girls thought or talked about. Since I am a still friend with some of those girls, I may have to ask them sometime about their thoughts forty-four years ago, in 1971.

In 1970, when I was thirteen years old, I attended First Church of Christ in my hometown of Ceres, California. I started going there after being invited by my friends Ron Megee and Wayne Dunbar. One Sunday I heard some of the other kids in our youth group talking about the upcoming summer camp at a place called Heavenly Hills Christian Camp which was somewhere in the Sierras. My interest was piqued so I began asking them questions about what church camp was all about. It was explained that camp was a week where kids would go, live in cabins, play games, swim in the river, sing around a campfire and study the Bible.

I was smitten with the thought and wanted badly to go. The only problem was I was from a single-parent family whose mother struggled to house and feed four children. It cost twenty-five dollars to go to Heavenly Hills and I knew that there was no way my Mom could afford it. When asked if I was planning to go, I mentioned this huge obstacle. Someone told me that a certain man in the church would pay a kid's way if the kid asked him personally. His name was Bob Jessup and he was one of the church elders.

I strongly desired to go to camp but I was mortified to ask for such a large sum of money from someone, especially a total stranger. It seemed a shameful thing to do. However, I really wanted to go because it sounded like such a great week. So, one Sunday morning I asked someone to point out Mr. Jessup to me. Then, I followed him all around the building in an effort to get him alone so I could ask him. I would have died if anyone heard me soliciting him for such a large sum of money.

Finally, I saw my chance. He went into the restroom and I prayed as I entered the door behind him that no one else was in that bathroom. I was so relieved to see only the two of us in there! As he stood at the urinal, I made my pitch, saying I had heard that if I asked him to pay the fee for me, I would be able to go to camp. He did not seem upset that I had asked him this, despite the surroundings or the task he was presently performing. He smiled and said, "What is your name?" I said, "Stan Faddis." He replied, "Well, Stan, you are going to camp." I cannot describe how happy I was. It was the greatest thing that had ever happened to me.

I look back on that event as one that set in motion another event that has forever changed my life. Several weeks later, our youth group went to Heavenly Hills Christian Camp in a caravan of vehicles. Camp was every bit as exciting as I had been told it was. Sitting around the campfire that week with everyone, I listened to a missionary who had been serving the Lord in Africa talk about Jesus Christ in a way I had never heard before. I went forward to answer that missionary's altar call to accept Jesus as my Lord and Savior. The following day I was baptized in the swimming hole at the river. Six years later, when I was nineteen years old, I moved away from Ceres to attend San Jose Bible College where that missionary man was now the president of the college. His name was Woodrow Phillips.

I am now fifty-eight years of age and to this day I credit both Bob Jessup and Woody Phillips for my life change. Woody's preaching was made available to me by Bob's generosity, which sent this poor kid to church camp.

As I have previously mentioned, I was not a good student; I hardly ever attended classes during high school. I recollect that in my freshmen year at Ceres High School, I received all F's on my report cards, even in PE. I don't remember if my mom tried to correct this poor behavior, but even if she had tried, I would have defied her. Even though I had no self-esteem, I did have a strong personality, which included denial and stubbornness. I now look back on that time and can see how dysfunctional I was. At the rate I was going, I would never amount to much of a contributor to society and I didn't care. My self-pity ran deep and wide.

Halfway through my junior year, I was kicked out of Ceres High for poor attendance and a (well) below grade-point average. School officials banished me to Argus Continuation High School across town. Most people presumed I was dumb and unable to handle school as a result. Prior to leaving for Argus, I was administered an IQ test so that, I guessed, it might be determined just how dull-witted I was. Several days after I took the test, the teacher who proctored the exam called me to his office. He advised me he wasn't supposed to reveal my score to me but felt it was something I that should know because he knew that I thought I was stupid and I should know the truth. He advised me that a person with average intelligence scores in the 90 to 100 point range on the test. He went on to say I had scored a 135, which placed me in the "gifted" range.

Argus was a "work at your own pace" school. After being told that I was not dumb, but was in fact pretty smart, I dove into the schoolwork at Argus where I remained for my junior year. I recollect that I left Ceres High with a grade point average of 1.3 (a low D average). At Argus I got straight A's. Although I felt good about being smarter than most, I still had little esteem for myself, mostly because of my obesity.

A couple of months into my return to Ceres High for senior year, my counselor Miss Pando called me to her office to discuss my future high school career. She sadly told me that, even if I excelled the rest of the year, I would not have enough credits to graduate with my class that June. I was given two options: stay an extra year or take an exam to get a General Education Diploma (GED). Back in those days, taking the tests for a GED was only allowed for those who were eighteen and older. The exception was to attend a High School Equivalency Program (HEP) to study for the GED and, once the staff felt a student was ready, the five GED tests were attempted. I did not want to go to school another year so I opted for the HEP.

Before I speak about my departure from high school, I need to insert the following item. Because I had so little confidence in myself, I figured that girls would not want to date me, so I didn't ask. I was mortified by the possibility that I would be turned down if I had asked. It was safer to not hope or ask a girl to go on a date with me. I feared rejection so much. I had one date in high school with a fellow classmate. It was for Senior Prom. Her name was Kathleen. Neither of us had a date for this very special night so our mutual friends convinced each of us to go together. I was excited and so I overdid it. I showed up at her house in my cool 1966 Chevy

Impala Super Sport to pick up Kathleen. I brought with me a corsage, which was fine. The "over the top" part came from the box of candy and bottle of perfume I also gave to her. I really can't say I had a great time that night and I don't think she enjoyed it much. The fact that it was arranged really put a damper on the night for her, I suppose, and me also. Nonetheless, the night was the highlight of my high school experience date-wise and I left shortly thereafter to go to HEP.

I arrived at the program, which was on the University of the Pacific campus some thirty miles north in Stockton, California in January 1975. The HEP classrooms were at the back of the campus near the football field in two Quonset huts. The program accommodated sixty students at a time and most of the attendees had been there for several months. Some had not been able to pass for a year or more. The enrollment was all Hispanic and African-American kids. I was the only white student during my time there. Because of this, I learned much about being discriminated against for my skin color. The HEP students lived in the various dorms on campus and I bunked in an all-male dormitory with a Hispanic guy whose name I do not recall. One day, this tough kid from Fresno named John came to our room and advised me that he was moving in because he wanted to be with his "home boy" and that I would be relocating to his dorm across campus where he had a room to himself. I am certain that the HEP staff was not aware of the new living arrangements for John and me but I didn't care. Having a private room was great news and it only got better when I learned my new dormitory was co-ed. I was seventeen and living in a dorm with a lot of girls who ran around half naked on their way to the bathrooms. It was a teenage boy's dream.

I sometimes went to the student union or the gym to play in pick-up basketball games. Everyone I came into contact with there (outside the HEP) assumed I was a university student and I played along. When asked, I said I was a freshman and that my major was in electrical engineering, something I had heard another student say. It's a good thing that no one asked me which professor I liked best!

My stay at UOP lasted a mere six weeks which is how long it took me to ready for and complete the five tests--Math, Social Studies, Science, Reading and Writing. Upon my departure, program officials told me I had scored the second highest test marks in the history of the program and had completed it quicker than anyone before me.

I so much loved my mom and was protective of her in many ways. I tried not to worry her with my behavior in the community (other than school performance). For instance, I always called her when I was out running around to tell her where I was because I did not want her to fret. However, these calls were often lies because I was usually not where I claimed to be. Fortunately for me, she always believed my lies and never checked my story.

Another painful thing for me in high school was that I didn't fit in with any particular group. I was in Band but was a lousy cornet player and not considered a part of that clique. I wasn't an athlete, a farmer, a stoner or an intellect so I didn't fit in with those groups. I wanted desperately to be accepted and "belong" but it wasn't so. On the other hand, I had a great sense of humor and made my classmates laugh a lot. This allowed me to navigate any group, but only temporarily. Needless to say, my humor was often self-deprecating. I made fun of myself for two reasons: to make people laugh and to beat everyone else to any punchline that targeted me. The bottom line was that I was an outsider and I didn't like it. This knocked down my already low opinion of myself to a new depth. Sometimes I made plans to "hang out" with some guys who said they'd come to my house to get me. I'd wait on the front porch for them to get there. More often than not they would not show up. It hurt because I was loyal and would sit there and wait for an hour or two. Later, I'd learn that they had forgotten me or had decided not to come and get me. It hurt deeply to be so low on their list.

One of my faults was that I liked to shoplift which began in the sixth grade. The thrill of taking something that wasn't mine was exciting and the sense of satisfaction of a successful theft was sweet. I recall vividly the very first thing I stole was a Hershey's Chocolate Bar with Almonds from Richland Market. I took it out to the peach orchard behind the store and savored every bit of it. I stole a lot from that store and some of my favorite prizes were Hostess Fruit Pies, which I believe cost nineteen cents at the time. Some of my classmates at Whitmore School and I occasionally walked downtown after school to steal stuff from Ceres Drugs including candy, writing pens and Magic Markers. I have no doubt that I introduced them to shoplifting and they would probably not have tried it had I not tempted them.

Our family didn't have much money so I thought I should do my best to do some type of work so that I could help Mom out financially. For several years between the ages of twelve and sixteen, I had a paper route, throwing newspapers for the Modesto Bee. The Bee paid me sixty cents a month out of each subscriber's two-fifty subscription fee to deliver the paper to their front porches six days week. I usually had about one hundred customers for which I earned sixty dollars a month. Other jobs I held included picking blackberries in the summer, working as a tractor driver during the peach season and selling stuff door to door such as JR Watkins products and newspaper subscriptions after I quit my paper route.

At age seventeen, during my (half) senior year in high school, I worked for Paul's Rexall Drugstore as a clerk and delivery boy. My shoplifting career continued during this time and being on the "inside" made stealing so much easier. It was during the six months that I worked at Paul's that I committed the biggest theft of my life. Each weekday I reported for work at 5:30 p.m. I would go to the back of the store and gather the prescriptions from the pharmacist I was to deliver that evening and map my route. I then went to see the store bookkeeper, who gave me the deposit to take to the bank which I would put into the night drop box. There were always two envelopes, but on one evening in December 1974, there were three of them. I boxed everything up, went to the delivery van and drove toward the Bank of America downtown as I was supposed to do. Part way there I got to wondering why I had three deposits to make that night. I pulled the van over and opened the zippered bank bag holding the envelopes. The third one was obviously different than the two usual ones. I honestly do not know why I decided to do it but I opened the envelope and found it had personal checks and $956 in cash inside. I decided to keep the envelope and I stuffed it into my pocket after which I deposited the other two at the bank. That familiar feeling of excitement came over me, more strongly than ever. I was scared but having all that cash was a powerful feeling and I began to think of all I could do with it. I naively hoped I would not get caught. The hope was bolstered by the fact I was soon going to quit work at Paul's and leave town to finish high school in Stockton. I burned the checks at the Ceres High

School football field and buried the money under the home team bleachers for a couple of weeks. Don't ask me why I did this at the school because I don't recall.

In late January 1975, a Ceres Police Officer named Louis Arrolo contacted me about the missing money. He said everyone who had access to the money was being investigated. I was very afraid I was caught but tried my best to remain calm while we talked. I, of course, denied stealing the money. He said he wanted me to take a lie detector test if my mother consented to it since I was under age eighteen. I told him I would comply but that I was leaving Ceres the following Saturday to go and stay with an uncle in Arizona and asked if we could do it before I left. I guess this must have convinced him I wasn't the thief and I never heard from him again.

One of the good things I did with the stolen money happened the Christmas of 1974. As I have said, we were poor; Mom did her best to give us everything we needed and some of the things we wanted. She spent little money on herself. One thing we could count on getting for Christmas was a package of socks and underwear. Well, that year, I took my youngest brother, Kevin, Christmas shopping in downtown Modesto. (There were no malls in those days). I had previously bought a cheap money clip, put $150 in it and placed it in my pocket. As Kevin and I walked down J Street, I tossed the money into a sidewalk tree planter when he was distracted. I said, "Hey, what's that?" pointing to the planter. Kevin picked it up and we counted the money. He had no clue that I was the one who had thrown it in there. When we got home, we told Mom about our "find" and gave her the money for Christmas. One of things she bought for herself that year was a vacuum cleaner, which she desperately needed. We kids received some nice things that year as well as the usual socks and underwear from JC Penney.

In the interest of full disclosure and to show how much I craved female companionship, the first twenty dollars of that stolen money was spent at a massage parlor in Modesto. It was the first of hundreds of dollars I have squandered at massage parlors, whorehouses and on streetwalkers. I became aware of prostitutes and brothels early in my life from my uncles who talked about them to one another and to me. My Uncle Jim once told me he had been a bouncer at a brothel in Susanville in the 60's. My Uncle Moe, with whom I went to live in Phoenix after I finished high school, introduced me to brothels. One night, he took me to the dog races and gave me some sips of his mixed drinks, making me pretty drunk. As we drove back to his house, he asked me if I had ever "been with a woman" (as in having had sexual intercourse) and I told him I had not. He asked if I wanted to be and I said yes. So, we drove to his liquor store, which had a three-bedroom house on the property. Uncle Moe explained he rented the house out to a pimp for a low cost and discounted booze. In exchange, Uncle Moe was allowed to visit the whorehouse with his guests for no charge. He took me inside and, at age seventeen, I gave up my virginity. This experience set up my sexual behavior for some time thereafter. I made a number of visits to brothels in Nevada in subsequent years including the infamous Mustang Ranch. For me, a person who feared rejection by women, it was wonderful because prostitutes never say "no." I don't blame anyone but myself for the poor choices I have made, but I wonder if I would have done these things had my first sexual experience not been in a whorehouse.

I lived in Phoenix for several months working at a McDonald's and caddying at the Phoenix Country Club a few blocks from my uncle's home. My Uncle Bill, whom I mentioned earlier, and his family lived nearby in Mesa. He was a bar musician and was extremely talented. He had a distinctive voice and could play guitar better than anyone I personally knew. Unfortunately, he squandered his talents due to alcohol abuse. One night in the 1970's, his band was playing at a bar in Mesa. During a break, two guys called Uncle Bill over to their table. They told him how impressed they were with his singing and playing. They said they were preparing to take their band on tour and believed he would fit right in, offering him $500 a week and his expenses. He declined, saying he didn't want to be away from his family as much as touring required. The two men turned out to be Willie Nelson and Waylon Jennings.

Before I went to live with my uncle Moe in Phoenix, I asked a girl who lived around the corner to go on a date. She was a year younger than me, was pretty, sweet and I liked her. I got up the nerve to ask her out because she was overweight, like me, and I figured my chances of being rejected were less because of that. That night, we went to the Ceres Drive-in and ended up in the backseat of my car. I was still a virgin and she was too, I presume. We began to make out and touch each other. I tried to talk her into having sex with me but she would not do it. The following week, I left to go to Phoenix and when I returned several months later I contacted her. By that time I had lost my virginity at the brothel. We went on another date to the drive-in and shortly after the movie started she threw herself at me and begged me to have sex with her. Now, one would think that I would be all for it. However, I had no desire to engage in sexual relations with her even though I did not really understand at the time what was holding me back. She got mad about it and told me to take her home, so I did. Several weeks later, I found out she was pregnant by a guy several years older and who wanted nothing to do with her or their child. It dawned on me that this girl was fishing for a guy to be a father for her soon-to-be-born baby. I firmly believe that God, knowing that I would have married her even though I knew I was not the father, but just because I had had sex with her, kept me from having intercourse with her that night when she offered herself to me. I came to believe that God had other things in mind for me so He protected me.

By the time I returned to Ceres to live with my mom, I had turned eighteen and had little ambition. I worked here and there at jobs I no longer can remember. I landed a decent job at Westinghouse Electric Supply Company (Wesco) in Modesto, working as a shipping and receiving clerk in the warehouse. I also made deliveries of electrical supplies to local companies that purchased our products. One of these companies was the Hershey's Chocolate factory in Oakdale, California. Does anyone else see the irony of this and my theft of one of their candy bars when I was eleven years old? Anyway, Hershey's policy was to not throw away blemished candy that didn't make it to the packaging phase. Instead, the imperfect candy was placed in plastic bins and set around the plant for employees and delivery people to eat and take as much as they wanted. I'm here to say that there is nothing tastier in the candy world than a Reese's Peanut Butter Cup that is only two or three hours old. This wasn't good for me due to my self-indulgent personality and lack of control. I probably gained twenty pounds from eating all that free candy.

Once I got the job at Wesco, I wanted to move out of my mom's house as soon as I could. I reconnected with a friend from high school, Doug McConnell. We played on a men's softball team together and, after talking about it for a while, we rented a two-bedroom apartment on Tully Road in

Modesto. In the months I lived with Doug, I began to spiral downward spiritually and emotionally. In some ways, I was doing well in that I had a full-time job, an apartment and all the freedom I had craved. But I also began to drink and party a lot. I started running with some of the guys on our softball team as well as a guy I had known since fifth grade. His name was Dave Stiffler and we were good friends. Dave had started smoking marijuana in Junior High, something I refused to do back in those days. My first experience with smoking weed came when I was eighteen and another friend talked me into trying it. From there, I experimented with amphetamines and LSD and I drank--a lot. I could easily consume one or two cases of beer in a weekend. Stiffler and I hatched a plan to become big-time marijuana dealers. He knew where to buy large quantities of it in Arizona and he trusted me to be his partner. However, before we could launch our operation, I got second thoughts about the venture as well as how I was living my life.

During this time in my existence, I recall thinking that I had little ambition to the point that I had decided there was no way I was going to get up each day and go to a job site. Being a bum was so much easier and I thought it suited me fine. I also remember thinking that, even if I was fortunate enough to find a woman who loved me and we had children together, there was no way I had the will to support them. In my mind it was too much work. Then, something happened that caused a major turning point in my life.

Chapter Three

One Friday night in September 1976, a friend and I each bought a pint of Jose Cuervo Gold Tequila and went to a football game at our alma mater, Ceres High. I was pretty drunk by the time we got there and, as we sat in the stands, I saw my childhood friend, Ron Megee, along with several people I did not recognize come walking in. Ron, who I had known since we were ten years old, had left Ceres to attend San Jose Bible College and I hadn't seen him for many months. He introduced me to his friends, one of whom was named Dave Baker (I'll have more to say about him later). Another guy I spoke to was named Tom Adams. He was several years older than me and it seemed like he was able to see into my soul. I can't really explain this other than to say he could tell I was spiritually troubled. He encouraged me to get back on track in my life without being judgmental. This was all in about the five minutes that we talked.

The next morning I woke up and laid in bed awhile thinking about my life. I was a Christian, yes, but I certainly was not producing any fruit of the Spirit and was only living for myself. I was extremely self-centered. However, I concluded that I didn't feel guilty about my lifestyle. After giving it further thought, I began to think my lack of conscience was due to the Holy Spirit abandoning me and I became worried. I did not want God to turn away from me and I came to the conclusion that I must drastically change my life.

However, I knew well my weaknesses and also knew I had no willpower to change if I stayed in the area. I concluded that I had to "run away" to a healthier place. The only such location I knew of was San Jose where Ron was living. So, a couple of weeks after that football game and the experience of having Tom Adams "look into my soul" I called Megee and asked if I could visit him for a few days to check out the situation. I went over there to spend a few days with Ron and his roommates at the 781 apartments on South 11th St. Originally, I had planned to just move to San Jose and find work, but in the few days I was there I discovered that I would have a chance at attending college. In my ignorance, I believed that I would be ineligible to go to college because I just had a GED. However, I learned that the school would accept me on academic probation and so I made the decision to become a college student. This was quite an undertaking for me because I had no money, a poor history of being a student, and a mom who was unable to help me out financially. It was suggested to me by someone in church leadership at Ceres First Christian Church that should I ask the elders for assistance. I did so and received enough money to pay registration fees and tuition for the first semester of classes. Later, I was able to get some student loans and my plan to graduate was to attend school one semester, then work the next semester, alternating each until I graduated.

Upon my arrival at San Jose Bible College for the winter term in 1976, I was assigned to live in the boys' dorm on campus, Beach Hall. School officials thought that it was a good idea to put me in a room with another new student named Doug, who was from Turlock, which is about ten miles from Ceres. There was never a more mismatched set of roomies than Doug and me. He was a very quiet, shy and introverted person who was in bed every night by nine. I was loud, rowdy and didn't want to end the days so I stayed out late. He was studious. I was not. In the beginning, college was the same as high school for me in that I goofed off, cut class, didn't study much and neglected to do my homework until the very last minute, if at all. I spent most of my time socializing and being entertained. And speaking of socialization, college was so much better for me than high school. Suddenly, I was among people who accepted and liked me for who I was. I immediately began dating fellow classmates, girls who were more interested in what was on the inside of me instead of how I looked on the outside. My humor and friendliness overcame my fatness and my self-esteem quickly grew.

The first couple of years at SJBC were so fun and full of activities. It seems like my friends and I were always on the move, hanging out in the boys' and girls' dorms, the cafeteria or the library. Many times we went to one of several restaurants like Denny's to study through the night. Another favorite destination was Farrell's Ice Cream parlor in Eastridge Mall. One night in Farrell's I was goofing off, trying to amuse everyone. I put the opening of a water glass up to my mouth and sucked on it until it attached. I held for a long time because my friends were laughing the whole time. When I took it off, I had a dark ring around my mouth, which was even funnier to them. It was a hickey! I looked like the cartoon character Fred Flintstone. The bruise stayed with me for several days. Hahaha. Very funny, Stanley.

We spent time on the quad area playing volleyball or building human pyramids. We often played pick-up basketball games in the gym. Many trips were made "over the hill' to Santa Cruz, its beaches and the Boardwalk. It was such a carefree time in my life.

Shortly after I enrolled in college, a friend asked me if I wanted to go to a Christian rock concert. I could hardly believe it because I didn't know there was such a genre as Christian music. I loved rock music! Some of my favorite bands included the Eagles, America, Heart, Crosby, Stills Nash and Young, the J. Geils Band and the Beach Boys. I was so happy to learn that there was Christian rock. The first show I saw was a guy named Randy Stonehill. One of my college professors, Jim Crain, headed up a company called Star Song, which put Star Song Radio on the air and brought Christian musicians to the Bay Area.

I had developed an interest in photography in high school and so I asked Jim if I could shoot some of the shows Star Song hosted. He said he didn't mind, and so between 1978 and 1992 I was one of the primary Christian music photographers in the Bay Area. I shot hundreds of pictures of bands including DeGarmo and Key, Phil Keaggy, The Imperials, Larry Norman, Daniel Amos, Sweet Comfort and Petra to name a few. Over the years I became friends with Larry Norman and Randy Stonehill. A few of my photos were published in *Contemporary Christian Magazine*. The music artist I became closest to is Bob Bennett whose music speaks to me deeply. Bob has performed two house concerts for Linda, our friends and me. As you may recall, he wrote the foreword for this book. I deeply love this man, his music and his heart for God. I thank Star Song for introducing me to this great music.

One time (around 1978 or 1979), several fellow students and I talked about how great it would be to invite a Christian music artist to the school to perform in the gym. We tossed around a few names and decided we should get Keith Green who lived in Tyler, Texas with his wife Melody and their children in a commune called Last Days Ministries. Keith had been a child musical prodigy and had gained fame at a young age, appearing on the Jack Benny Show as well as the Steve Allen Show. He played the piano as well as other instruments, wrote his own songs and performed them. After his conversion to Christianity, Keith became an evangelist who was determined to bring the message of Christ to the masses.

It was a long shot that he would come to San Jose to play a concert but we decided to try anyway. I went to my apartment, got on the phone and dialed 4-1-1; I asked the operator if she had a listing for Keith Green in Tyler, Texas. She said, "I have a Keith and Melody Green, is that the one you want?" I said, "Yes ma'am!" I called the number. Melody answered and I asked to speak to Keith; he came to the phone. I explained to him I was a student at San Jose Bible College and that we hoped he would come to perform a concert for us. He asked, "When?" I gave him the date and he said he would be there. All he asked was for us to provide a grand piano and to take an offering to pay for his expenses. On the day of the concert, Keith and two other guys pulled into the parking lot in a Jeep Cherokee they had driven all the way from Tyler, 1,800 miles away. It was so exciting and the concert was great! At intermission we passed the hat for the offering. As you can imagine, we didn't collect much from the audience of college students but Keith did not complain. After the show, he and his traveling companions jumped into their Jeep and headed home.

On July 28, 1982, Keith, a couple of his young children, and several friends of Last Days Ministries died in a small plane crash. Keith was twenty-eight years old.

I made friends with a lot of people, many of whom I have kept touch with these many years. A few of these guys are lifelong friends and we communicate all the time and sometimes get together. To me, this is one of the most precious things about going to San Jose Bible College. It was small and intimate.

I previously mentioned Dave Baker so I will go into more detail about our friendship. I first met Dave who was from Yamhill, Oregon at Ceres High when he came with Megee and the others to watch the football game. Dave caught my eye due to his appearance that night. He was tall, blond, slightly built and wore a trench coat and a rubberized cowboy hat although there was not a cloud in the sky. He was kind of goofy and funny. We met again when I moved to the dorm and, after I lived with Doug in Beach Hall for a term, I moved into a room with Baker. We later roomed together in an apartment a block from the school with a couple of other guys. We became good friends. The summer after my first year, Dave took me in his green Chevy Vega to Central Point Oregon where he dropped me off at my girlfriend Debbie Crumm's house. He was on his way home for the summer. We had a couple of interesting episodes on that twelve-hour trip. First, his Vega died without warning as we merged from Interstate 680 to Interstate 80 at the Cordelia Junction in Fairfield, California. We coasted to the shoulder, got out and looked under the hood. Dave was a pretty good mechanic but neither of us could figure out the problem and could not get the car to restart. After a few minutes, Dave suggested that we lay hands on the Vega and ask God to "heal" it. We each put our hands on the car, bowed our heads and prayed aloud seeking divine intervention. Dave closed the hood and said, "Let's go." I doubted that prayer had worked but complied. Dave turned the key, the car started right up as if nothing had ever been wrong and off we went. It was so cool! We whooped and hollered, thanking Jesus for the miracle.

The second event occurred about twenty miles up the road on Interstate 505. It was very hot that day and we saw a canal alongside the highway. We agreed to take the next exit at

Allendale Road. We stopped, parked and prepared to jump into the refreshing water. We stripped down to our skivvies and then I decided I didn't want to get back into the car with wet underwear so I stripped all the way and jumped in. Dave did the same in spite of the fact that vehicles were driving past not one hundred feet from where we were swimming. People in cars couldn't see us, but a couple of truckers in big rigs got an eyeful.

The last event happened on Interstate 5 north of Shasta Lake as we drove through the Siskiyou Mountains. There was major construction during this time as Cal Trans was widening the highway. Traffic was funneled through those tall orange plastic tubes anchored in heavy black rubber bases. I was driving at the time and watched as Dave reached over into the back of the car and retrieved a baseball bat. He instructed me to get as close to the cones as possible. He rolled down his window and stuck the bat out to knock some of them over. Although we were going sixty miles an hour, neither of us considered what would happen when he made contact with the first cone. His hand was slammed into the doorpost but he held onto the bat, quickly pulling it back. A sane person would stop at this point, but no one had ever accused Dave Baker of being sane. He told me to slow down, which I was able to do because there were no cars behind us. At about thirty miles per hour, Dave knocked about ten of those tubes down and we then sped off. We were idiots.

The guys I associated with were very interested in the girls at school and we spent a lot of time pursuing these females. Although we didn't know or appreciate it at the time, we were very fortunate to be among such a wonderful group of girls. They were kind, pretty, smart and loved God. Of course, we gave little thought to all this but we did know we were very blessed. Some of the girls resided on campus and some were local residents who still lived at home with their parents.

One girl was Leann Desmond and she was from San Jose, still living at home. She was a beauty and several of the guys wanted to get her attention. One of our male friends, Curt Pernice, who was a San Josean, knew Leann and told us not to bother. According to him, Leann was dating some college football star and had no time for us. Everyone heeded his words except for Dave Baker who secretly began to court her. He didn't want the rest of us to find out and perhaps join in the pursuit so he didn't say a word about the fact he was dating her. Dave was a doofus and Leann was the cream of the crop so no one ever suspected the relationship until Dave finally admitted they were dating. I didn't even know and I was his roommate!

The following summer, Dave, who played on the SJBC basketball team, was invited to go to Taiwan with the Sports Ambassadors to play ball and evangelize there. I was going to go home for the summer to work in the cannery and save money for the next quarter's tuition. Dave told me he didn't want Leann to be lonely while he was gone. He asked if I would mind coming over to San Jose from Ceres once in awhile to keep her company. He said I was the only guy he trusted to do this. I was honored that he asked me to do this and of course I did it for him. It wasn't much of a sacrifice, believe me. On June 17, 1978, Dave and Leann were married at Los Gatos Christian Church and they are married to this day. Take a guess who the big man was that stood next to Dave as his best man that day.

Landing in college, let alone a Bible college, was the last thing I would have thought would happen to me, but it was the best thing that has occurred in my life. It was there I met my wife, developed friendships that have lasted for more than thirty years, and earned a college degree that placed me in a career I could not have had otherwise.

Additionally, Bible College was where I had some of the greatest experiences of my life--hanging out in the quad on the campus, socializing with some of the best people in the world, and doing fun things together was wonderful for me. Living in the boys' dorm, Beach Hall, allowed for plenty of good times. We played pranks on each other, went to movies together and learned how to live in community as we drew closer to God in this atmosphere. San Jose was about thirty minutes from Santa Cruz and we made many trips there to hang out on the beach and cruise the boardwalk. It was such a rich time in my life and honestly I did not appreciate it as much then as I do now.

One man I must mention is Lewis Mick. His wife, Minnie, was the school's librarian and Mr. Mick was SJBC's handyman at the time. He was in his eighties, I believe, and was a never-ending source of frustration to me because he always seemed to be on my back about something. I'm sure, to him, I was nothing but a hooligan and he was continually correcting me regarding my behavior. For instance, he never failed to jump on me for wearing my hat inside a building, telling me it was disrespectful. To him, I was too loud and did not respect my elders. He never failed to point this out to me.

Outside the school's library was a book return receptacle that was about the size of a U.S. mailbox some of us remember used to sit on the corners of neighborhood streets. Mr. Mick had built it and painted it to look like a large yellow and brown bird. People would put their borrowed books into the bird's beak and these dropped to the bottom of the box.

One night, some friends and I decided it would be funny if we put the bird where it belonged--in a tree--because that's where birds live. We hoisted the bird up into a tree by the cafeteria and the next morning we saw Mr. Mick standing there looking at it. He was not happy. He went to get a ladder, climbed up on it and got the bird down. A lot of people were standing around watching him perform this task and when he got the bird out of the tree he looked directly at me and glared because he knew without a doubt I was responsible for putting the bird up there.

One day, I had had enough of Mr. Mick always correcting me, so I asked him, "Mr. Mick, why are you always on my back?" He replied, "Because you are one of my Ceres boys and I want you to be the best person you can be." His answer puzzled me because I could not recall ever knowing Mr. Mick when I lived in Ceres. It was not long afterward I learned he was formerly the pastor of the church in Ceres from which I hailed--First Church of Christ. It made me laugh because I also learned Mr. Mick had been the pastor of that church in 1932 which was twenty-five years before I was even born. As I look back on this, I realize having Mr. Mick always on my back helped mold me into who am now. Our interaction was brief but important.

Back in the summer of 1978, I bought a car from my mother's friends for three hundred dollars, and it was one of the coolest vehicles I have ever owned. It was a 1964 Chrysler New Yorker and somewhere along the way one of my friends dubbed it the "Stanmobile." To this day, whenever someone talks about that car, it is ALWAYS referred to as the Stanmobile out of respect and awe. The car was huge, white, had blue-green cloth seats and a back shelf big enough to curl up on to take a nap. The Stanmobile sported a rectangular steering wheel and a push- button transmission. Under the hood was a 413-cubic-inch engine with a Holley four-barrel carburetor. I once took it to a parts store in Modesto to have the store's owner look at the engine because I needed a part. The man's name was Charlie Bell and he was a local racing legend who drove Dodges, aka Chrysler products, aka Mopar. Charlie popped the hood and upon seeing the engine, his eyes got big. He reached over to the engine head and wiped some grease off a small area near the carburetor revealing an X stamped into the metal. He told me the car's 413 cubic inch engine was not ordinary; it was a HIGH PERFORMANCE motor. Awesome!

I already knew it was fast because of one of several events I will now recount (admit to). Once, when I was back at home in Ceres, I was performing some routine maintenance on the Stanmobile. My two young cousins Larry and David were helping me. We took a quart-sized bottle of Rislone Engine Treatment, which one is supposed to add along with engine oil. Instead and purposely, I filled the secondary two barrels of the carburetor to the brim with Rislone. The third and fourth barrels do not kick in until a certain amount of acceleration is achieved. The carb is fitted with a butterfly valve that stays closed until the extra power is required. This allowed the Rislone to stay in the top of the carb until I punched the gas pedal, causing it to open and dump the engine treatment into the motor. Upon doing this, a huge, sustained cloud of thick black smoke would gush out the car's tailpipe causing much laughter inside the Stanmobile.

We added the Rislone and slowly drove into the nearby country and onto a little-traveled road. David and Larry urged me to "punch it" and so I did. However, just as I did so, I noticed a yellow Corvette come around the corner behind us at the same moment that massive black cloud was emitted from the Stanmobile. This appeared to anger the driver of the 'Vette and he gave chase, I assume to do us bodily harm. We took off at a high rate of speed, slowing only enough to negotiate turns. The guy chased us for a couple of miles until we got into a long, straight stretch of road and I floored it. Within a few moments, we were doing 120 miles per hour, and as I watched in my rear view mirror, the Corvette shrank to a Hot Wheels-sized car and was soon far behind. Pursuit terminated. We all cheered. The Stanmobile had outrun a Corvette!

The other Stanmobile confession involves an incident that occurred in San Jose. Five of the "dudes," Mark Thompson, Mike Huskey, Bill Dobos, Rick Criscione, and yours truly, drove in the Stanmobile to a local theater to see a movie titled *The Driver*. It starred Ryan O'Neal and the Internet Movie Database (IMDb) offers the following synopsis: *"The Driver" is a specialist in a rare business: he drives getaway cars in robberies. His exceptional talent prevented him from being caught yet. After another successful flight from the police, a self-assured detective makes it his primary goal to catch the Driver. He promises remission of punishment to a gang if they help to convict him in a set-up robbery.*

We loved the movie and excitedly discussed it as we drove in the night back to the school campus. I remember saying how much I wished I could drive like Ryan O'Neal did in the movie and how cool it would be. Upon arrival at the school, one of us had a great idea. I don't remember the genius that proposed it, but all of us liked it so we executed our plan, which was for me to show off my wicked driving skills. Now, at the back of the campus was the Earl E. Arneson Memorial Field, a softball diamond that had fallen into disrepair due to lack of use. The field was on the lower part of the property next to Coyote Creek and it had a road we drove down and on to the outfield of the diamond. The grass was about a foot high and wet. I punched the car's accelerator and we started doing 360's all over the place. Our fun was increased when we noticed several cottontail rabbits eating the rich grass. We chased them, but had no traction and no control of where the car would go as we were spinning around and around and sliding sideways. (No animals were harmed in the course of this event).

After a few minutes of spinning donuts and chasing furry creatures, we drove back up the road into the parking lot of the Beach Hall Boys' Dormitory where a guy I'll call Dorm Dad whose true name shall not be spoken in this story out of respect for his anonymity, met us. He was accompanied by a couple of other guys who lived in the dorm and they all appeared quite worked up. Our northbound merriment only moments earlier quickly turned south as Dorm Dad lectured us five scalawags on our bad behavior, disregard for authority and poor Christian witness. We reasoned we had done no damage other than causing the outfield grass to lay down where the car tires had skidded across it. I told him we did not drive on the infield even though we knew no one used the softball field anymore. After he chewed us out for a while, we were dismissed and we drove away. The dudes agreed it was no fun being reprimanded like that; however, the thrill of our reckless abandon that night was worth the dressing down we had received. To this day, it only takes two words (The Driver) to make the five of us recall and laugh about it.

I respected and feared all my college professors; respect because of their knowledge and dedication, and fear because they expected much of me. I often worried I could not fulfill their requirements well enough to pass their courses.

Dallas Meserve frightened me the most. He taught a Life of Christ class among other subjects and was a tough man to please. He sometimes acted sour but he was actually a nice man who liked to laugh. A good story about his rigorous teaching and tough manner was seen by a large group of freshmen including me on the first day of Mr. Meserve's Life of Christ course. From the front of the classroom, he held up a Bible and announced that the translation in his hand was the ONLY one to be used for his classes. It was a New American Standard Bible. A freshman in the back of the room raised his hand and Meserve called on him. The kid had a thick southern accent and we later learned he was from somewhere in the Deep South. He said, "Mr. Meserve. What do you think about the Scofield Bible?" We all watched as Mr. Meserve, who was bald, turned red from his cheeks to the top of his head. He told the naive freshman, "You can bring your Scofield's right down here and toss it into the trash can by the door!" End of discussion.

A professor I really like is Jim Crain who, among other courses, taught Homiletics, the art of preaching. Jim's easy manner and friendliness was magnetic and his classes were popular. He is a man of great fortitude evidenced by the lame and sometimes inappropriate sermon illustrations his students formulated. One such illustration was offered as to how the Word of God was given to man. The budding preacher likened it to conception, describing how the female egg travels down the fallopian tube to be met by the male sperm. I wasn't there but I'm told Professor Crain's jaw hit the floor. Now in his seventies, Jim still teaches at the school which is now called William Jessup University after its founder, and is located in Rocklin, California. I've heard Jim is the most popular teacher on campus.

My favorite professor was Michael Jonathan Bowman who taught Western Civilization and Religious Art among other things. He was really tough, quick-witted and I wanted to be just like him. Mike cared about his students and it was cool that he was only about ten years older than my peer group and me. It was clear he loved teaching and was good at it. One of the biggest boosts to my self-esteem occurred in class one day when Mike used me as an example for one of the points he was making. He said, "Stan Faddis is an inherently intelligent person." I'll never forget Mike Bowman, whom I regard so highly, believes I am intelligent. I think of the moment often. By the way, I had to look up the word "inherently" after class to know what it meant. True story.

I went through quite a few phases of change during my college years that began in November of 1976 and ended in May 1984. I began as an immature nineteen-year-old who knew very little of the world did not know for certain how I was going to support myself and really was not concerned about it. I wanted to be successful but had no plan laid out for such success. I worked at various jobs during those years including delivering flowers, manufacturing wicker bathroom furniture, silk screening t-shirts, machining metal cylinders and working at a company that made blueprints for circuit boards. I did not last long at any of these jobs because I was easily bored, lazy and not a very dedicated employee. I often called in sick so I could go have fun.

I went from being a single person with few needs to being a married man-child in 1980. I admit that, even at age twenty-three, I was still a boy who didn't want to leave Never-Never Land. I quit school and had no plans to finish, primarily because I was still only a sophomore after four years of going to classes on and off. Linda and I got our first apartment in Modesto. She worked at a steady job for a company called Nasco West, a school supply store, and I slipped into my pattern of working intermittently. I was employed for a while at a convenience store and also crossed a picket line at Gallo Winery to work as a forklift driver during a strike for a short time. Upon being hired, my fellow "scabs" and I were promised we would be kept on even after the strike ended. However, surprise, surprise, this did not happen. We were quickly escorted out of the building a couple of weeks later when the union strikers returned to their jobs.

Sometime around November 1980, an opportunity presented itself that was very attractive to both Linda and me. We were offered a position as the caretakers of Heavenly Hills Christian camp in the Sierra Nevada Mountains. The camp was very dear to me as it had been the place where I had met the Lord and been baptized years before. So we moved up there and lived in a doublewide mobile home to care for the property and host incoming groups from churches throughout the Central Valley for winter retreats. It was a great job for us, which we both enjoyed. Unfortunately, we had been led to believe by the camp's director who was the current caretaker this would be a long-term job for us but soon found he was not being honest about it. It turned out he wanted a particular older couple for the job but they weren't able to come until the following spring. So, after a few months, we were terminated. Faced with no plans for the future, Linda and I decided it might be best for me to go back to college, get my degree and then go into full-time youth ministry as I had dreamed about doing.

In April 1981, Linda and I drove to San Jose for her interview at Downey Savings and Loan. She had several friends who worked there and her interview was just a formality as they had already procured the position for her. Within a few weeks we packed up our stuff at the camp and moved to San Jose where we lived for a short period of time with some Bible college friends.

One block from the school was a seventeen-unit apartment building that housed mostly SJBC students. As I looked for a place to live and a job, I learned that the apartment building (referred by the tenants as the 781's due to its address on South 11th Street) had no vacancies but the longtime manager, a woman named Grace, was ill. A couple of her adult children were managing the place until she was well enough to resume her duties. I heard that Grace probably wouldn't come back and that her kids were not very good managers, not taking care of business and smoking marijuana all the time.

I found out that the owner of the apartments was Harrett Mannina, Sr., an attorney. I made an appointment to see him. I told Mr. Mannina I had heard Grace was sick and might not be able to work for him anymore. I pitched myself for the position, pointing out the work I had done as a caretaker at the camp, that I would shortly be returning to school, and had experience handling money. Mr. Mannina said he'd keep me in mind for the position should it open up but that as long as Grace could do the work, she would remain as his manager.

A couple of weeks later, Grace passed away, and I was hired to do the job that consisted mostly of collecting the rent, keeping the peace and performing light maintenance. There was a plumber and handyman retained by Mr. Mannina to do the stuff I couldn't do. As managers, we got free rent, which was great because it saved Linda and me about $700 a month. We managed the 781's for ten years, from 1981 to 1990.

When we first began managing the 781's, we didn't have any children (Daniel came along three years after that) so our financial needs were not much. With Linda working full time at the bank, we were set. We struck a deal with one another. I told Linda if she worked while I finished school and let me concentrate on my studies, she would never have to work again. We wanted her to stay home with any children that came along and I would support them. It all worked according to plan. Three years later, Daniel was born on April 26, 1984, the day after Linda resigned from the bank. A month later I graduated and began looking for work to fulfill my promise to her.

Although I didn't realize it at the time, moving away from Ceres and enrolling in college was the primary step that changed the course of my life. In the beginning, I had so little confidence in myself that I gave no thought to actually graduating. It was the pattern of my life to not set goals. I'm not sure why but can guess that either no one had taught me the importance of it or maybe I didn't want to disappoint myself or others by setting personal goals I would not likely accomplish. In all, it took me eight years to earn my bachelor's degree. On May 26, 1984, Linda, our son and my mom were all there to see me walk across that stage and get my college diploma.

Chapter Four

Prior to graduating, I believed I was a shoo-in for several youth ministry positions throughout the state. This belief was based on the fact that I had a several senior pastors tell me, "Stan, once you get your degree, I want to hire you as our church's youth pastor." They told me how impressed they were with me and how well I related to the young people. I was sure I would be offered a job but was unable to land work as a youth pastor. All the promises of church positions had suddenly disappeared, causing me to be deeply discouraged. I looked for work in the church for four months and came up dry. I was desperate to get a job so that I could be a man and make good on the promise I had made to Linda three years prior about her staying home with our children.

One day I was talking to my friend and former college roommate George Gardner, who said he had heard Santa Clara County Juvenile Hall was looking to hire some extra-help employees. The title of the position was Group Counselor and it paid $9.00 an hour to start. As we later learned, the title is somewhat a misnomer and a more accurate name for it would probably be Correctional Officer. George and I applied and were joined by our friend Mark Thompson who was also seeking employment. I don't recall if Mark was working somewhere else at that time; however, George was employed as a mail carrier for the United Postal Service lugging mostly junk mail door to door. He couldn't wait to get a different job.

A few days later, Mark and I were called in for an interview. Upon arrival at the Hall (as it is referred to by most everyone associated with it), we were escorted to the office of Dexter Albright, a Probation Manager, who greeted us warmly. There were some very nice scenic photos hanging on his wall that I commented on. Mr. Albright said he had taken the shots and then we spent the next half hour talking about photography. As Mark and I discussed this later, we wondered to ourselves when we would be called into the interview with whoever would perform that task. It seemed like we were just having a chat with this man.

Then, Mr. Albright said, "Okay, call me tomorrow and I'll let you know when to come in for the mandatory eight-hour observation and to pick up your keys." He gave us his direct phone number. I responded by saying, "What about the interview?" He said, "This was the interview and I've decided to hire you both." Wow! Talk about informal and easy. However, it also didn't allow us to learn anything about the job duties we would be expected to perform or the hours we were going to work.

Nonetheless, I was very excited to get the job and be paid $9.00 an hour on top of that! At 8:00 the next morning I called his number but he didn't answer and there was no voicemail. I called every half hour but the phone just rang and rang. Mark was also calling from his apartment with the same results. Needless to say, I was impatient and angry that Albright failed to pick up. Finally, at 3:30 in the afternoon, a female answered my call. I asked to speak to Mr. Albright, to which she replied, "I'm sorry, Mr. Albright no longer works at this facility. He was transferred to the boys' ranch in South County." What? I thought, "This cannot be happening!" I needed that job and now I didn't know if I was going to get it. Fortunately, after explaining to her why I was calling, she gave me the number of another manager whom I contacted about the position. I found out later that Albright had done something that got him demoted and reassigned. I never heard any specifics. Perhaps it was his interviewing technique. Hardy har har.

Upon making contact with the other manager, I was scheduled for the aforementioned "observation" which was set for the following day. So, on October 31, 1984, yes, on Halloween night, I went to Juvenile Hall for the 3 p.m. to 11 p.m. shift to learn about the job. The full-time Group Counselor I first spoke to advised me that, since it was Halloween, "The kids might be a little more misbehaved than usual." No joke! Those kids were going wild, yelling out their room windows, making scary noises and acting out in a number of ways. Honestly, I almost changed my mind about working there because of this. I was accustomed to church kids who could also get wild and crazy, but were not as scary and out-of-control as these kids. However, I survived the shift and decided to give it some time, to work there until I could find a church to hire me. I planned to give it no more than a year and I hoped it would even be less than that. Well, I finally left the Probation Department on April 1, 2011—twenty-seven years later. George was also hired around the same time and also stayed for twenty-seven years before retiring.

For many years thereafter I was angry with God for not placing me in full-time ministry in a church. Finally, I realized He had put me in a place where I could minister to young people who could benefit from having good role models. He knew my skills and life experiences were best used in probation where the spiritual and emotional needs are amplified. Further, every two weeks I received a paycheck, had excellent health benefits, which was very comforting, and I, unlike so many of my former college mates, did not have to be concerned with getting fired by church leaders who might become dissatisfied with their youth pastor or because the wind was blowing the wrong direction that day. God knew I needed the stability of steady employment and a pension as well as health coverage for the current time of my life during which I have been so unhealthy.

Working as an Extra-Help employee did not necessarily mean we only worked part of the time. Almost immediately, I began working forty hours a week, earning seven hundred dollars in a two-week pay period. Soon, I was working sixty to eighty hours a week and earning up to $2100 a month. I scrambled to get hours because the more I worked, the more I earned and the better I could support Linda and Daniel. Our financial situation was made better by the fact that we were still not paying rent, as we were the apartment managers of the 781's. The best part was that Linda was home being a full-time mom.

Extra-Help workers do not receive benefits; however, a few months after I took the job, I was offered a "provisional" position that included benefits, and in June 1985, I was hired full-time. It was a Union job and I became a member of Local 1587, which meant a good raise to about $13.00 an hour and full Kaiser, dental and vision benefits as well as a $500,000 life insurance policy. This base salary equaled about $27,000 a year, but there was a lot more to be made from all of the overtime that was available to me. During my thirteen years in the Hall, I worked many seventy- to eighty-hour weeks as I was driven to provide the best living I could for our family. Heather was born in August 1985 and Holly in May 1987. Speaking of Holly, I thank God for that Kaiser insurance policy. She was born six weeks prematurely and spent the first month of her life in the Intensive Care Nursery. She weighed less than four pounds when she was born. It was estimated our hospital bill would have been over $100,000 for her stay, a debt that would have been financially crippling.

Although we were called Group Counselors (GC's), the job was more that of correctional officers, or as some people referred to the job, Turnkeys. Our primary task was to protect the kids, also called "minors," under our care, from hurting themselves or others. The others included their fellow cellmates, nurses, teachers, kitchen workers, custodians and Group Counselors.

During employment as a GC in the Hall, I mostly supervised sixteen and seventeen-year-old boys. My largeness and the ability to act tough really helped me to do the job. My sense of humor was also a valuable tool, particularly my biting sarcasm. For each eight-hour shift, I worked with two or three other GC's to run the unit, depending on the population of that unit. Most of my years were spent in Units B1, B2 and B3, the "B" designating it as a boys' unit. B1 was the unit where the minors who had committed the most serious crimes were housed. These included violent crimes such as rape, armed robbery, mayhem and murder. Also housed in B1 were any minors who were waiting to go to the California Youth Authority (CYA) for committing felonies. CYA was the prison for minors up to age twenty-five. A minor had to have been committed to CYA prior to turning eighteen, but could stay until their twenty-fifth birthday at which time they usually were released on parole. On the other hand, those who had committed murder or other heinous crimes prior to turning eighteen could then be sent to state prison on their twenty-fifth birthday if the Court ordered it so.

Here is a job description from the Santa Clara County Probation website regarding the duties of Group Counselors:

> Assist in the supervision of a group of juveniles detained in a detention facility. Learn to organize and/or supervise leisure time activities, such as games, athletics, and crafts and encourage participation. Prepare observation or incident reports on detainees' attitudes, behavior, appearance, interests, skills, progress, and needs. Maintain security and safety of the facility at all times.

Since I left the Hall, the units we had then have been torn down and new ones constructed in their place. The three units I worked the most were identical in style and I'll try to describe them.

Upon entering the unit door from the main hallway one would see a long hallway lined with cells on each side. There were a total of twenty-six rooms, each designed to hold two minors, that had metal bunk beds attached to the back wall and a metal open box-like locker attached to one of the walls at eye level. The rooms were about eight by eight feet in size, painted a beige color, and the beds and lockers were metal gray. The exceptions were rooms 1 and 2, which were single bed rooms meant to house only one person. These held kids who were either a serious threat to themselves, were too violent, or had sexual issues that required they not be alone with the others. The beds in these rooms were made of a solid slab of cement and were the dimensions of a twin bed. All the bunks had a mattress that was approximately four inches thick. Each minor was issued two sheets, a blanket and a pillow.

At end of that hallway was a supply room on the right that was about ten by ten feet. To the left was a large bathroom that had three toilet stalls, three urinals, three sinks, a large circular sink and a five-sided shower post that had five shower heads so that many minors at a time could wash up. The shower was turned on and off by the GC behind the desk who could observe the bathroom as there was a Plexiglas wall that ran the length of the bathroom. Minors were let out of their rooms five at a time to take a three-minute shower and then perform the typical personal hygiene tasks.

Turning to the right out of the hallway was a large activity area which had a ping-pong table, a TV, fifty plastic chairs with metal legs and some three-by-five-foot tables used for writing letters and playing cards games, board games and dominoes. Through a locked door off that room was a large outdoor courtyard where the minors played basketball, volleyball or handball. There were a couple of flat benches to sit on at each end. The wall to the courtyard was also Plexiglas.

The chairs were lined up in a horseshoe configuration whenever the boys came out of their rooms to prepare to go to a meal or to school. This was called "set-up." Once all the minors were in set-up, one of the counselors went over what was expected of them on the movement to the next destination or activity. This was called "structuring" and all the GC's took turns doing it. Following is an example of a structure in preparation to go on a breakfast movement to the cafeteria in another building:

> Good morning gentlemen. As you know, we are getting ready to move to the cafeteria for breakfast. You will walk in a straight line with your hands at your sides. There will be no talking until you are seated and no

communicating with those in other units inside the cafeteria. Keep your hands to yourself and act like gentlemen. You're not allowed to bring back any food from the cafeteria so make sure you eat it all there. While it is okay for you to give away your food, it is not permitted that you pay off any debts that you may have incurred by betting on sports, which is against the rules in here. You will not take the food off anyone's tray without his permission. You're expected to keep your eyes forward and there will be no rubbernecking [looking around to stare at and flirt with the girls]. Eat quickly and don't let excessive talking slow you down.

Structuring was done prior to every group movement out of the unit to another destination on the grounds as well as before other activities such as going outside to the yard or watching a movie or TV show. Needless to say, structures could get very boring for the minors as well as the GC's because they were the same instructions over and over, day in and day out.

One day at home, I had a brilliant idea. I pulled out our cassette player/recorder, inserted a blank cassette cartridge and recorded a structure tape. The next morning I went to work with that tape tucked into my work bag. I advised the other GC's I wanted to do the morning structure that day and we got the kids out of their rooms into the setup position. It was the custom for the GC who was structuring to stand at the top of the horseshoe-shaped setup to give the structure. So, when it was time for me to do it, the kids and the other GC's wondered why I continued to sit behind the desk, reading the newspaper. After a pregnant pause, giving them all time to wonder what I was doing, I reached behind me and pushed "play" on the stereo system. I had placed the queued-up tape in the player while no one was looking. I then opened up the newspaper again. A few seconds later, my recorded structure began to play. It was the same old stuff in a flat monotone, making it even more boring and painful. The tape ran almost ten minutes and covered every instruction in detail. The other GC's thought it was a great idea. The word spread and GC's from other units borrowed it to play for their minors. It was such a hit that the tape was used every day for quite a while. The minors moaned loudly when it was played and they dubbed it the "Torture Tape" because it was so painful to listen to. Mysteriously, the cassette disappeared from B3 after several weeks and was never seen again.

The shifts in Juvenile Hall were broken down into three eight-hour segments--7 a.m. to 3 p.m. (Days), 3 p.m. to 11 p.m. (Swings) and 11 p.m. to 7 a.m. (Graves). Each of these shifts had different routines as dictated by what the minors were doing during a particular time period. On the Day and Swing shifts, when the kids were more active, three GC's supervised each unit. An extra GC was assigned if the population ran over a certain number. On Graves, there was one Night Attendant whose primary task was to check the rooms and let kids out to go to the bathroom for "head calls" when they knocked, asking to use the restroom.

The units I worked the most, B2 and B3, were designed to hold fifty minors each. However, sometimes the population could climb to the sixties. During these times, we had three kids to a room with the third one sleeping on two or three mattress stacked up on the floor.

A daily routine on the Day shift, Monday to Friday went like this: the first GC to arrive came into the unit from the main hallway and take a headcount as he or she walked up the unit hallway to the desk. If the count matched with that of the night attendant (NA), the GC signed off and the NA left to go home. By this time, the second and third GC's would have come in. As they moved toward the desk, they knocked on the doors to wake up the minors. They stored their personal belongings behind the desk. One went back to the end of the hallway and started popping (opening) doors a few at a time for the kids to come out and go to the bathroom to wash up. As those kids returned to their rooms to make their beds and dress for the day, a few more would be let out to begin their cycle. There was a GC popping doors, a GC standing at the doorway of the bathroom to watch and one GC behind the desk. This GC kept an eye on the activity area as the minors came from making their beds to the setup, ready to go to breakfast. Usually, the TV was turned on so they could be occupied.

Upon popping the last few doors, the hallway GC moved to the back of the activity area to monitor from that position as the bulk of the population was now in that area of the unit. B1 was the first unit to be called for breakfast. At about 7:30 a.m. the Control Desk (CD) gave them the green light to move from the unit to the cafeteria. So, B3 had a half-hour to count, awaken and wash-up and structure fifty minors before moving out.

Upon returning from breakfast, the minors went back into setup. One GC went down the hallway and the minors were dismissed four to six at a time to return to their rooms beginning with the farthest away from the desk. They stayed in their rooms for about an hour before being called back to ready for the school movement. They went to school between 9 a.m. and 3:30 p.m., four or five periods a day. They were broken into three groups and moved to their various classrooms in

another building. A fourth group met in the activity area with
an onsite teacher. There was a break for lunch with the minors
moving to the cafeteria the same way as at breakfast.

My first paid day on the job, I worked the 3 to 11 shift
in B3. As I walked down to the desk to meet my new
coworkers, I saw two men whom I estimated to be in their late
thirties or early forties, standing behind the unit desk, which
was about four feet high and eight feet long. One man was big
and the other one was short. Both looked to be Hispanic. As I
approached the desk, I smiled, held out my hand and
introduced myself. The shorter of the two put out his hand to
shake mine and said, "Hi, my name is Joe G. Martinez." The
big guy looked at me, did not offer to shake my hand and said,
"Sir, do see that hallway down there?" He pointed back to the
hallway I had just walked up. I said I did see it to which he
replied, "It's all yours for this entire shift. Stay down there, look
into the rooms every fifteen minutes, sign the watch sheets on
the doors that have them and let kids out of their rooms one at
a time when they knock to make a head call. Last, do not come
up here to this desk without first asking one of us for our
permission."

I found out later his name was Tim Valdez. He is of
Native American and Mexican heritage. He, like Joe G. was a
veteran GC. They had both been there over fifteen years,
working in the "trenches" as they referred to it. They took great
pride in running a tight ship, keeping even the toughest kids in
line, and were highly respected by the minors and the other
GC's. I was taken aback by Valdez's gruffness and felt he was
treating me like a third-class citizen. However, I quickly learned
two things . . . I was being trained by the best, and Tim Valdez
was a teddy bear. The way they did their jobs made B3 a very

safe place for everyone to be, and I was lucky to work many shifts with them. Their motto was "Tough, but fair." The kids feared and respected Mr. Valdez and more than once I heard a minor tell a newcomer to be careful not to "piss off" Mr. Valdez because he was one of the fiercest GC's there and he could really hurt a kid if he "restrained" him.

To explain . . . sometimes when things got out of hand like during a fight or when a minor completely refused to move from Location A to Location B, GC's had no choice but to physically lay hands on the offender(s). This was done by placing the minor in a certain hold and applying pressure on the wrist and/or elbow joint until the minor complied with the order to do what he was told. This is referred to as pain compliance. About a year after I started working in the Hall, I asked Valdez why the kids were so fearful of his restraints. I was curious because I had never seen him lay hands on any minor. Tim chuckled and explained that the whole thing was just a legend. He said he had restrained some kids early in his career and the reputation was set in place. He estimated he had not had to touch a minor in more than five years.

Valdez was able to keep his unit in line by his reputation as being able to put the hurt on a kid if he restrained them. This was in spite of the fact he had not touched a minor in many years. Reputation was the key for him. The kids gave it a second thought before starting a fight when Valdez was on the job.

In the first week of working at Juvenile Hall, I had a strange encounter with a supervising group counselor (SGC). I will call him Fred, which isn't his true name. He stopped me in the main hallway as I was walking to my unit. Fred said something like, "I know you are one of those Bible college guys we just hired. I want you to know that you are not here to proselytize these kids; you are here to supervise them." I thought it was kind of weird because I had never spoken to the man prior to that moment. I was puzzled by his instruction and wondered why he would even say something like that. About a week or two later I think I got the answers to my questions. On that day, two San Jose police detectives came to Juvenile Hall and arrested Fred. They escorted him out of the building, never to be seen inside there again. It was found that he had been carrying on an affair with a female minor he had met in Juvenile Hall. It was rumored he had set her up in a small apartment a few blocks away so he could visit her often. I believe now that he lectured me that day because he did not want me to mess up his future possibilities by proselytizing his future girlfriends. Certainly, the man lost his job and his pension. I believe he was prosecuted for having sex with an underage female.

At the beginning, it was somewhat intimidating to be inside a locked facility with fifty or so law offenders and only three or four staff. I knew it would be easy for so many of them to turn on the few of us, and even though there were other staff members close by if we needed their help, we could have been seriously injured before such assistance arrived. I also wondered if I could learn the job and do it well. My upbringing helped me because it taught me how to act like I was tough which is how I thought I needed to be perceived. However, I learned quickly that being tough but fair was the best way. If I showed respect, I got respect from the wards. I also wanted the kids to be better people and saw that I could teach some of them if they wanted help. I concluded that many of them did not have good male role models and I strove to be a good example.

Every day at work, there was a potential for something bad to happen, whether it be fights or suicide attempts or assaults, or even a riot which was preplanned by the minors. GC's at that time had no mechanical restraints such as handcuffs to neutralize minors. We only had physical means such as wristlocks, by which we removed unruly kids into their rooms, and our keys, to lock them up. When it was necessary and we were able to do so, kids were escorted to isolation rooms in other parts of the Hall. When things got too out of hand, it took a lot of GC's and sometimes our supervisors to jump in and help. So, the best thing to do was try our best to prevent bad things from happening. This was where some good old psychology came in handy.

I often worked with a man by the name of Paul Love, a soft-spoken man. He was body builder who had won some major competitions in his career. Now in his seventies, he is still involved in the sport by promoting shows in San Jose through his company, Paul Love's Silicon Valley Productions. One day I asked him why he never needed to restrain the wards. He was such an imposing figure; I presume that was deterrent enough. He said he had a technique he always used when it appeared a fight was getting ready to start.

When two minors squared off and started "woofing," Paul would tell them in his calm voice, "Gentlemen, stop. Step back." If they ignored him, he said again, "Gentlemen, separate yourselves." If that didn't work, he said he would remove his wristwatch and set it on the desk or put it in his pocket and take one step toward them. The result was always that altercation was terminated by choice of the two combatants. As a rule, the minors did not want Mr. Love to restrain them. He was intimidating without being a bully. They respected him and his physique very much.

One of the best ideas we concocted to keep the unit free of contraband was something we titled "Amnesty." On Friday nights one of the staff on the 3-11 shift made a new population chart, pairing roommates for the following week. We switched roommates weekly in order to keep the minors from getting too familiar and to prevent problems which might result from them getting on each others' nerves. On Saturday morning after breakfast, we had all the kids strip their beds and pack up their stuff by bundling it up in their sheets. They then came to the activity area into setup where they sat holding their belongings on their laps. Two six-foot tables were placed end-to-end and a GC was stationed at each of them. Beginning with the closest rooms, we called out the names of the two boys who would occupy the room that week, even assigning who would have the top and the bottom bunks. They brought their bundled sheets up which contained their stuff including gym shorts, pillow case, books, cards, pictures, magazines, etc. and spread everything out on the table where the GC's searched it. They were handed two clean sheets, a pillowcase and towel. They placed their dirty linen into the designated carts to take to the Laundry later. The boys then went to their rooms two at a time where they settled in by making their beds and arranging their possessions in their wall lockers. The process was repeated until all the minors were assigned a new room and their stuff searched.

Contraband was and remains a large problem in custody facilities. Juvenile Hall contraband included food (often smuggled from the cafeteria or from visits with parents), extra clothing (a t-shirt or underwear could be torn into strips that could be fashioned into a noose), anything that could be used to make weapons (tooth brushes, disposable razors, paper clips or any metal that had been broken off from something else), lotion and latex gloves (think about that one), and drugs smuggled back from the outside or given to a minor by a parent (it happens more than you'd think).

Although we were very good at room searches, the kids were better at hiding things as they had so much time to come up with places and ways to secret contraband. They saw it as a challenge and a victory if the GC's couldn't find whatever they had hidden. And because they were better "hiders," they were also better "finders."

This is where the amnesty program came into the picture. After the minors were moved into their rooms, we pulled them back out into setup. We announced that that day was an amnesty day and anyone who wanted to participate could do so. We told them, "We're going to send you back to your rooms right now, and we want you to look for any contraband that was left in the room from the week before. You have fifteen minutes to search. If you find something, bring it to the desk and you will be given a soda and candy bar. After the time is up, everyone will come out to watch a movie while we go to search the rooms. If anything is found, you will be disciplined for it. It doesn't matter if it was already there or not. You are now responsible for it." We did not do the amnesty program every week but when we did, it was always highly successful. The minors came back with all kinds of stuff that we probably would not have found. All it cost us was a can of soda and a candy bar for each of them. We were smart enough to know that some of those kids were turning in their own contraband so they could win a treat, but we didn't care because the rooms had been searched by the best and we got lots of contraband from them.

Chapter Five

I like to play practical jokes. I'm not one who enjoys scaring people, although I have done this on occasion. I just like to joke around and sometimes come up with some pretty good ideas. I also like it when others prank me, which indicates I can dish it out AND take it. Sometimes, I suppose my joking is just weird, but it usually gets a laugh and, to me, that makes it all worth it.

After George, Mark, and I had been working at Juvenile Hall for six weeks or so, we began to hear about an annual Christmas party that was hosted by one of the Juvenile Hall nurses, Lavonne. We did not get an official invitation to the party, but we reasoned that no one told us specifically that we couldn't go. We decided to attend and our goal, being the "new guys," was to make a splash. We knew that everyone would be dressed up in nice clothes, so we decided to arrive wearing togas. We found out the location of Lavonne's house and the time the party was to begin. We deliberately planned to arrive an hour late so we could get the most bang out our surprise. Prior to heading to the party, we stopped at Juvenile Hall and borrowed some white bed sheets. Using safety pins, we made togas and put them on. Our ensembles also included boots and hats that any cowboy would have been proud to wear.

As we approached the house, we heard the party going in full swing. We knocked on the door and Lavonne answered it. The look on her face said, "Who are you and what do you want?" Presumably, she did not recognize us, but after all, we were the new guys. She invited us in after we identified ourselves. As we entered the living room, we saw all the nicely dressed people staring at the three toga-wearing idiots. I said, "We were told this was supposed to be a toga party! The joke is on us!" It worked - we had made our mark and everyone thought it was great.

Sometimes my pranks were planned to make a point. One time a contractor broke the water line to the gymnasium fire sprinkler system. As a result, someone had to sit in the gym twenty-four hours a day in case a fire broke out so he or she could pull the fire alarm. It was a silly way to spend county money because anyone who worked overtime during the shift was paid time and a half. This meant some of us were making $66 an hour. This earned me about $528 per shift. I worked many graveyard shifts during this time. It took a long while for the contractor to fix the damage and get the sprinklers back online. I bided my time listening to music, snacking and shooting baskets. We couldn't sleep because it was important to stay alert (wink, wink).

One night I felt like making a point about the foolishness of spending so many taxpayers' dollars on this and getting some laughs at the same time. So, at about 10:45 p.m., I walked into Police Admissions to sign in for the 11 to 7 shift. I was wearing pajamas, holding one of my daughter's teddy bears, and sucking my thumb, and I had a baby blanket slung over my shoulder. Other people were either reporting to or leaving work so there was a lot of traffic through that area. Most of them cracked up at the joke and gave me knowing head nods. A new supervisor, Bret Fidler, who was getting off work at 11:00, saw me, causing his face to turn bright red. It was clear he didn't appreciate my humor. I thought he was going to send me home so I told him I had appropriate clothes to change into. At that time I did not know Bret very well. He and I have since become very good friends. We talk on the phone several times a month.

We came up with some pretty good ways to entertain the minors and ourselves during our shifts in Juvenile Hall. One thing that most people don't realize is how closely the kids watch the counselors either to observe one of them doing something wrong or trying to learn something about their personal life. They were also figuring out how to manipulate us. There were some very talented kids in Juvenile Hall, some of whom stayed there for months at a time. Some of them were good dancers, good singers and rappers, and some were very funny. One thing we learned was that kids spent much of the time, mostly out of our hearing, mimicking us. More than once, I walked by minors' rooms to hear them impersonating one of my coworkers or even me. I'd like to say that I was the originator of the following idea, but I wasn't. I believe that honor goes to my coworker, Randy Martinez. On one Saturday morning during some free time, while we were waiting to go to lunch, Randy stood in front of setup and said, "Who can mimic one of us counselors?" Several hands went up and it was on! Martinez said, "Who wants to get up here and do me?" Two kids raised their hands and Randy chose one of them. He told the minor, "You have three minutes to do your very best impersonation of me and then we'll give the other guy a chance. Whoever does it best will get a soda and candy bar after lunch."

It was amazing to watch those kids do perfect impersonations of Martinez. They had him down to his voice inflections, facial expressions and the things he commonly said. It was nothing short of hilarious and everybody in the place rolled with laughter. I thought it was great but then it was my turn. Randy said, "Who can do Mr. Faddis?" Three kids raised their hands and each in turn got up and did spot-on impersonations of me. I have to admit it wasn't as funny to me as those who had mimicked Randy; in fact, it was somewhat embarrassing. I think it took a lot of guts for them to get up there and do that but we also had pretty stiff spines to allow them to do it in front of everyone and then to reward them for it.

I suppose I need to admit that the kids were not the only mimics in the place. There was one supervisor there who had a distinctive voice and addressed most people as "my friend" when he spoke to them. Mr. Wesley Johnson was a tall African-American man who was well-educated, and he spoke as if he were. Anyway, I could mimic him pretty well and got a lot of laughs from co-workers when I did it. Of course this was never when Mr. Johnson was in my vicinity.

Part-time work is also referred to as "on-call." So, we were supposed to be available twenty-four hours a day, seven days a week. The rule was that if you were called to come in to work, you were expected to do so. If you refused, you had a mark put next to your name. Three such marks resulted in having your "sheet pulled." If your sheet was pulled, they did not call you to come into work for a couple of weeks. This was 1985 when answering machines were just coming on the market. Some of us thought we could circumvent the process by buying an answering machine. If the phone rang at home, we would listen to see if it was Juvenile Hall calling and would not pick up the line if we did not want to work that day.

I bought my first answering machine at RadioShack for $79. When I got home with it, I recorded my greeting. Wes Johnson was not one of the supervisors that would call part-timers to come into work because he worked in a different area. So, I felt very safe when I recorded my impersonation of Mr. Johnson on my brand-new answering machine. The recording went something like this, "Hello my friend! This is Wes

Johnson answering the phone for my good friend, Stan Faddis. Stan is not here right now and cannot take your call but please leave a message and he will get back to you as soon as he can." I then left our apartment and went to a beach party in Santa Cruz with a bunch of people from work.

When I returned home, I could hear my phone ringing inside the apartment. As I entered the living room and looked over on the kitchen counter where the answering machine sat, I noticed the red light was not blinking; there were no messages for me--yet. I really wanted whoever was calling to hear my Wes Johnson impersonation so I let the phone ring until it picked up and played the message described above. Here's what I heard, "Not funny, Stan. Not funny! This is Wes Johnson. Please call me as soon as possible."

Needless to say I was mortified. Not only was Mr. Johnson the first person to hear my hilarious greeting but also the only one who ever heard it on that machine. I immediately called the Hall and asked to speak to him. When he came on the line, I said something like, "So, Mr. Johnson, have I ever told you my philosophy of why people mimic other people?" He did not respond, so I rushed on and said, "I believe that we mimic only those whom we truly admire." About a millisecond later, Mr. Johnson said, "Well Stan, I used to do a very good impersonation of Adolf Hitler but I can't say that I admired the man." Ouch! I had no snappy come back to that one so I told him I was sorry and asked if I still worked there. He went on to tell me that, yes, I still had a job in spite of my extreme disrespect, and that I was being offered a full-time position. I erased that recording from the cassette tape, packed up the machine and took it back to RadioShack for a refund. After all, I didn't need it anymore since I was no longer a part-timer.

I need to mention that at least five years later, I was talking to Mr. Johnson and Sue Robertson, a female supervisor, in the cafeteria. As we chatted, she started laughing at some funny thought she had. She said, "Hey, Wes! Remember that time Stan left a message on his answering machine mimicking your voice?" Even then, Wes did not think it funny and he ignored her.

One graveyard shift, I was working in Police Admissions when two Police Officers brought in a kid for suspicion of drug sales due to the fact he was from the Los Angeles area and had a large sum of money on his person. They found no drugs, but since he did not have a parent to whom they could release him, he was brought to Juvenile Hall as was the procedure. He would be held in the Hall until one of his parents could come up to get him. As was customary, they removed the handcuffs and handed me a large envelope containing the items they had removed from his pockets upon his arrest. The nurse came from the clinic to do her routine check on the minor and then cleared the officers to leave.

I processed the minor, which included inventorying his belongings, asking him certain questions such as his name, age, address, parent contact information and the like. When asked what he was doing in San Jose, so far from home, he admitted he was here selling drugs. He went to say he had just sold the last of them and was going to take a bus home to LA. He said he was lucky not to have any drugs when the cops stopped him. He thought he had attracted their attention by looking so young and hanging around the bus station waiting for his bus.

I was somewhat astonished to see he had over $1000 in cash in the envelope handed to me by the police. When I commented on him having such a large amount of cash, the minor said, "F**k that. Those cops ripped me off for $5000!" He went on to say he had over $6000 when they stopped him. He claimed he got this money from selling "a lot of cocaine" he had brought up from Los Angeles. They told him they were going to take the money and that he had better not "snitch" on them because no one would believe him anyway. They further stated he was lucky they were leaving him with $1000.

I reported all this to my supervisor who said it was the minor's word against two police officers and there was nothing that could be done about it. I would really like to think the kid was lying but I also wonder what benefit he thought he would get for making it up. I want to believe the officers wouldn't stoop so low as that, but things like it do happen. The incident has crossed my mind many times over the years and I still wonder what is the truth.

Some of the GC's in Juvenile Hall were quite colorful characters but Larry Armstrong led the pack. He was of German descent and had worked as a Night Attendant at the James Boys' Ranch for many years before being hired as a GC in the Hall. I first met him when he was in his fifties. The man was an opinionated know-it-all and often brusque. Both the minors and staff disliked him for his surliness.

At this point, I should give the reader some information regarding court cases and other information regarding the justice process. In the adult court system defendants are arraigned, tried and found guilty. However, in the juvenile system the youthful offenders are called minors. In the event that a crime is committed a petition is filed. Minors are not "tried" or "convicted"; they are "adjudicated" and the equivalent of being found guilty is the "petition found true."

During the years I worked in Juvenile Hall, some minors who were adjudicated and their petitions found true were allowed to serve their sentences in Juvenile Hall on the weekends. We referred to them as "weekenders" and they came into the Hall on Friday at 5 p.m. and were released at 5 p.m. the following Sunday. During the mid-90's Juvenile Hall became overcrowded (one of many times) and so on some Fridays, the Presiding Juvenile Court Judge would instruct Juvenile Hall to refuse admittance to minors on that particular weekend due to the overcrowding.

On one such Friday, Larry Armstrong was working alone in the Police Admissions area where officers brought in the new admits and where minors reported for the weekend. A fifteen-year-old minor walked in the door to be admitted and Larry told him, "We're not taking weekenders; the Hall is overcrowded." The minor said, "My Dad just dropped me off and is heading for Tahoe for the weekend. He'll be back Sunday to get me. No one is home." (This was in the days before cell phones so the kid couldn't just call to have his father come back to pick him up). The Supervising Group Counselor (SGC) on duty was in the cafeteria across the campus as was routine during mealtimes. Larry did not bother to call him about what he should do. He just made a unilateral decision to turn away the minor. Armstrong told him, "It's not my problem. You can't stay here this weekend."

The minor told Armstrong he had no way to get home and that the doors were locked anyway. Armstrong reiterated it was not his concern and gave the minor bus money to get home. The minor subsequently went home and broke a window to gain entrance to his residence. Being left unsupervised for the weekend, he took the keys to his father's other car and went for drive. Upon making an illegal turn on his joy ride, a San Jose Police Officer stopped him. Upon investigation, the officer learned his tale. He cited the minor for Breaking and Entering, Auto Theft and being an Unlicensed Driver. He transported the minor to Juvenile Hall where he was admitted for committing the new offenses.

That Sunday, the minor's father came into Police Admissions to pick up his son. He was told that the boy was now in custody for new charges and could not be released. Imagine his anger when he found that his car was impounded, which would cost him $250 to get back, and that he also was out the cost to repair a broken window.

Fortunately for the Department and Larry Armstrong too, the minor had not been hurt while driving his dad's stolen car. I presume Armstrong was reprimanded in some way, but I'm not certain how. I do know that he was never allowed to work in Police Admissions from that day forward.

It seemed as if Armstrong was happiest when he was complaining about something or someone. As previously mentioned, he had worked for many years at the Boys' Ranch in Morgan Hill. More than once I heard him griping about a woman he had worked with down there. He despised her for unspecified reasons and often called her "that stupid b***h." He also ranted that she had falsified her job application and did not have the education she claimed on her application. People wondered why he loathed her so much or why he cared about her educational qualifications. By the way, Armstrong claimed he had his Doctorate in Rocket Science or something like that. Some folks wondered why such a highly trained person was working in the juvenile system.

At any rate, his ranting about the woman piqued the interest of an SGC who pulled Armstrong's personnel file to take a look at his job application submitted years previously.

He had listed a university in the Eastern United States where he acquired his degree many years prior. Out of curiosity, a Probation Manager (PM) contacted the school to verify Armstrong's date of graduation and the degree he received. The school official advised the PM that there was no record of Armstrong earning a degree from the school. In fact, no records could be found that he had even been enrolled there. The result was that Armstrong was immediately fired and he lost his entire pension--approximately twenty-five years' worth down the tubes.

By far, the most fun I had in Juvenile Hall was when I worked with Dario Lerma. He was a veteran of the Hall and the good times we had made the eight-hour shifts feel shorter. The kids loved him even though he made them toe the line. His humor was the best and we spent a lot of the time joking. The primary thing I learned from him was how to interact with the minors. Through him, we had fun with the kids, but never at their expense. I also learned a lot about Mexican culture from him, things like work ethic and familial customs. One day he brought in to work some burritos his wife Ramona had made for us. It was my first taste of *chorizo con papa y huevos* burritos (sausage, potatoes and eggs). Sometimes he would button up his flannel shirt to the top and act out being a "lowrider" calling everyone "esse" and "homes."

Dario was about ten years older than I and had worked there for ten years by the time I arrived. He is Mexican, born in El Paso, Texas and raised in Corcoran, California where his family worked as farm laborers. He told me, "I'm a cotton picker" and he wasn't joking for once. He moved to San Jose to go to college, after which he got a job in Juvenile Hall in 1974. Four years after I was hired, Dario was promoted to

Probation Officer. The Hall was not the same after he left. Dario's hobby, it seemed, was almost constantly trying to pull someone's leg. During downtimes on the 7 a.m. to 3 p.m. shift, while all the minors were in their schoolrooms in another building, we often listened to oldies on the radio. Dario, being my elder, really knew his oldies, or so I thought. We played a game in which we tried to name the tune, the artist and the year it was released. More than once, I caught him making up bogus facts and we always laughed about it. He once told me he used to write things on the bathroom wall like, "If you don't like someone who works here, put their name below."

Juvenile Hall had a program called the Foster Grandparent program. Each weekday from about 10 a.m.to 2 p.m. elderly men and woman came to the units to spend time with the minors. It was meant to provide a homelike environment for the kids and it was great. The program employed some of the nicest folks. The Foster Grandparents were paid a small stipend of about $2.00 an hour to talk to the kids and play cards, dominoes, or board games with them. The ladies in the girls' unit sometimes taught crocheting. Admittedly, not all of them were the stereotypical grandparents. Grandma Sally was a wicked card cheat; Grandpa John would only play poker with the kids; and Grandma Gertrude often had the smell of an alcoholic beverage about her person.

One of the best pranks Dario ever played on me occurred on the 7-3 shift in Unit B4 where Grandma Gertrude was assigned as a Foster Grandparent. On that day, all the kids were at school, and Dario and I were sitting behind the desk, which was U-shaped, and about four feet high. Grandma Gertrude, who had seemed a little tipsy to us that day, was sitting at a table in the activity area, playing solitaire. Dario called out to her, "Grandma!" and ducked down so she couldn't see him. She looked over toward the desk to see me sitting there with this stupid look on my face. I was embarrassed and told Dario to knock it off. He stayed down until he thought she wasn't looking anymore. He popped back up and said in a louder voice, "Grandma!" and ducked again, laughing quietly. She looked at me again and the only thing I could think of to say was, "It wasn't me, Grandma." She went back to playing cards and again Dario hollered, "Grandma!" and went back down. This proved too much for the poor woman. She looked at me and yelled, "What the f**k do you want?" I stood up, grabbed Dario and picked him up high enough for her to see him, telling her it was Dario that had been calling her. He busted up laughing but did not apologize for messing with her. A real riot he was.

Another thing about Lerma was that nothing ruffled his feathers and he was always calm. He didn't let anything get to him and he rarely raised his voice to the kids. In short, he was very laid back, or it was a very convincing act. One day we were working in B4 on the day shift. All the kids were in school and we were sitting behind the desk with the radio playing. We had about thirty minutes to do nothing before we walked over to pick up the school groups and escort them back to the unit. Dario was reading the *San Jose Mercury News*, holding up the paper so it obscured his view, which was no big deal since there were no kids to keep an eye on. I leaned back in my chair and closed my eyes. The bright fluorescent light above us was irritating so I reached over, grabbed a clean towel from the cabinet and draped it over my eyes. A small amount of light leaked in at the side.

We sat listening to the music and chatting for about twenty minutes. Then I saw some movement through that small opening of the towel. I pulled it off to look, and there stood our SGC with her hands on her hips, glaring at us and not saying a word. Her name was Lynette Takamoto, a short, stocky woman of Japanese descent. Dario still had the paper in his face and he had no clue she was there. I reached over and slapped him on the arm. "Dario," I said, "Ms. Takamoto is here." Lerma looked over the top of the newspaper and said, "Oh. Hello, Lynnette." Then he raised the paper back up and went back to reading. Me? My mind was racing and I worried we had been "caught." Ms. Takamoto told Lerma to put down the paper and said, "I just walked all the way up that hallway without either of you seeing me." I said, "Sorry." Lerma said nothing; he just sort of smiled. She advised, "Something like this had better not ever happen again." She then turned and walked out without another word. When she had exited the unit and was out of earshot, Dario said, "A man can't take a nap or read the paper in this place without being hassled." He went back to his paper. Mr. Unflappable.

After being promoted to Probation Officer (PO) and moved to the other side of the building in 1997, I continued to play pranks. I'd walk into an empty elevator and stand facing the corner, my back to the door. I then would ride it up and down the four floors of the building, waiting for people to get in. I did not acknowledge them or look around. In almost every case, the person did not say anything or ask me if I was okay or not. Since I did not look at them, I didn't know who was in the elevator with me. I surmise that, on at least a few of those occasions, there were some management types or maybe even the Chief Probation Officer. As I said, this is probably a character flaw--messing with peoples' minds. It was harmless, but probably not too smart in that particular case.

Sometimes I sat in the one stall of the second floor bathroom at JPD. I could see through a crack between the door and the frame so I was able see the reactions I got. I'd make weird sounds like I was in pain or crying. Most of the time people would quietly chuckle, but other times they couldn't keep from bursting out in laughter. On several occasions, when I walked out of that bathroom, the guy I had been messing with would be standing in the hallway, waiting to see who had been in the stall. My favorite times were when a fellow officer brought a minor in to get a urine sample from the kid. The officer tried to keep it together and the kid would try his best to provide the sample, but my sounds made both tasks almost impossible.

Speaking of taking urine samples, I was in there once with a minor I did not know after being asked by his female PO to obtain his sample. The kid was having a tough time of it so I asked him if he was reluctant because it would turn up positive for drugs. He strongly denied it even after being pressed by me several times. While this was going on, a fellow PO named Bruce Henry came in and heard our interaction. I looked at Bruce, who was also a big jokester, and immediately knew he had something in mind. Bruce said, "Hey Stan. What did you think about that training we had the other day on how to see positive urine samples by holding them up to the new light they invented?" I played along saying it was very cool. Just then, Bruce looked up at the old run-of-the-mill fluorescent light in there and said, "Hey! It looks like they've already installed one of the lights in here." By then, the kid had produced a small sample and handed me the bottle that I dropped into the baggie and sealed. We asked him again if it was dirty and he said it was not.

Bruce suggested we "test" it right then and there, so I held up the sample to the light. Bruce stood behind me and we made a big show of peering at it. Bruce stated, "Oh man! That sure looks like a dirty test to me." Simultaneously, we looked at the minor who hung his head in shame and said, "Yes, sirs. It's dirty. I smoked some marijuana last night."

By far, the best prank I ever played at JPD (and was almost played back on me) was when I hatched up an elaborate plan. I had been advised by management that I was being moved administratively to Adult Probation, which is not uncommon, and it was going to be a nice change of pace for me. During the two weeks prior to the move, I played several pranks on my coworkers that led to the grand finale. One of my best friends, Paul Luera, had a lot of interesting items in and around his desk. These included a poster of John Belushi from the movie "Animal House," a large Harp beer mug and a stuffed armadillo. One day I typed a memo to him that stated it was from the Deputy Chief Probation Officer. It said the DCPO had noticed the "unprofessional" appearance of Paul's desk and he had until 5 p.m. to remove items or he faced severe disciplinary action. I put the memo in Paul's mailbox and waited for him to return from the field. I was at my desk in the adjacent bay when he came in and went to his mailbox. I couldn't see him but I knew he had read the memo because he cried out, "Oh no! I'm in big trouble!" I was busting up with laughter as I heard him scrambling to clean up his desk. He was making little sounds of distress and I couldn't bear to make him suffer any longer. I went to his bay and confessed I had typed the memo. His look of relief was priceless.

I played several other jokes and, as a result, one coworker, Wendy, asked me if I was going to play one on her. I told her it wouldn't work if she was expecting it so the answer was no. However, a couple of days later, I came up with a big prank for which I needed her help so I told her this. She excitedly said she really wanted to do it, even though she hadn't heard the plan and I did not think she would go along with it, because it involved me pretending to kiss her "against her will" in front of everyone in the unit. Even after I revealed it to her, she agreed to play along.

Wednesday was "goody day" when someone in the unit brought in treats for us all to share that morning. Since that was the day and time everyone was there, the prank would be played to the largest possible audience. As we all gathered around the food, I gave Wendy the high sign. She nodded that she was ready. I got everyone's attention by saying, "I'll be leaving soon and I'm going to miss you all. But Wendy, I am going to miss you most!" I reached for her, took her in my arms and kissed her on the lips. Someone gasped but there was complete silence otherwise. Wendy acted very upset and said, "I'm going to the fourth floor!" This meant she was going to go complain to the Powers and she stormed out of the room, headed for the elevator. This announcement shook the others because they knew that good ol' Stan was in big trouble. My coworkers went to their desks and our supervisor, Ned, retreated to his office having contracted a sudden and severe migraine. I followed him and watched as he sat down and cradled his head in his hands, rubbing his temples and moaning a bit. He said, "Stan! What have you done? How are we going to handle this?"

The plan was for Wendy to be gone for a minute or so and then walk back in for the big reveal that it was all was just a prank. She didn't come back and I began to worry. It crossed my mind that she could easily have gone to Management to make a sexual harassment claim. She had witnesses and this event could have cost the county a lot of money and me my career. I began to panic. Just then, Ned's phone rang. The caller ID showed that a manager, Glenn Arima, was calling Ned. He answered it, listened and said, "We'll be right there." He hung up and said we were needed on the fourth floor. My life flashed before my eyes and I knew my days as a probation officer were over.

In the elevator ride up, I confessed to Ned the whole thing was a practical joke that Wendy and I were both in on and asked him if he was in on something with Wendy to turn it around on me. I prayed he would say yes, but he denied it and I knew he was telling the truth.

We walked into to Mr. Arima's office and saw Wendy standing there with her hands covering her face, crying. Now I was terrified. Then, Wendy peeked at me through her fingers and smiled. Instant relief. Arima, sitting at his desk, said, "Stan, are you causing trouble again?" He was smiling. Wendy, Ned and I walked to the elevator laughing about the whole thing and I complimented her on getting my goat in the process. We agreed that Ned and I would go back to the unit and that Wendy would come in a minute later.

As Ned and I entered the unit, all seven of the other PO's were heading out the door to escape the trouble. It reminded me of cockroaches scattering when the light is turned on. Ned announced, "Freeze!" and everyone stopped. He said, "Mr. Arima wants Incident Reports from everyone on what just happened here." My dear friend, Paul Luera, who had been approximately four feet away from the "crime" said, "I didn't see anything!" A female coworker vowed that she was going to kick Wendy's a** for telling on good ol' Stan, the nice guy. Just then Wendy walked in. The seven glared at her. She walked toward me and we both laughed and gave each other a high five. It took a second, but our coworkers realized the whole thing was a prank. Pauly said it was "genius." I said, "Shame on you probation officers for taking the side of the perpetrator against this poor victim." We all laughed and then went about our day knowing that their goats had been gotten and that all was right between Wendy and me.

In the Bible, the Book of Ecclesiastics states, "There is nothing new under the sun." However, I cannot imagine the following prank is something anyone, besides my cohorts and I, have done before or since.

It was 1986 and I was hanging out a lot with Rick Criscione and Mark Thompson. Rick gave the credit to Mark and me for coming up with the idea that was nothing short of brilliant. These two guys went to and graduated from San Jose's Yerba Buena High School in 1976. In 1986 they made plans to attend their ten-year class reunion. They were talking about it one day and discussed the deadline for sending in their money, what to wear, etc. Because I had attended both my five and ten-year reunions of Ceres High School's class of 1975, I was regaling them with tales of how fun such reunions can be. At one point, I wistfully stated how great it would have been if the three of us had attended Yerba Buena so we could go to the reunion together.

Suddenly, a light bulb lit up our devious little brains. I could go with them by impersonating one of their classmates. Both Rick and Mark said they knew everyone they had attended school with and they concluded they'd be able to come up with a person whose identity I could hijack.

We sat down with their senior yearbook and started our search. The task was not as easy as it first appeared because at

Yerba Buena, white people like myself were the minority. Then, there was the challenge of finding a guy who was big and tall like me. As fate would have it, we found one guy who fit our bill and Rick and Mark did not remember him. So much for knowing "everyone."

The guy's name was Mitch Cunningham and the resemblance was not very close. He wasn't as big as me and I think he had blondish hair. We reasoned that many people change in the ten years after high school but this was really pushing it. I believed the prank was too good to pass up so we went for it. I mailed in my money for the cost of the reunion and identified myself as Mitch Cunningham.

We spent quite a bit of time talking about it and how we would handle the inevitable threat of someone blurting out something like, "Hey! You're not Mitch! He died in 1983 from a drug overdose!" Or something to that effect. The scariest thought was that Mitch himself would show up and blow the deal. My plan was to lie and say, "I'm the real Mitch Cunningham!" Needless to say, we were all pretty nervous about it, but it was just too good to not try.

A fourth guy, Rodney Williams, who had also graduated with Mark and Rick, was let in on the prank. On the evening of the event, we all went to the Saint Claire Hotel on First and San Carlos streets to begin our night of lies and celebrating "our" ten-year reunion!

I recall us approaching the sign-in desk and identifying ourselves. I was a bit worried because I thought there was a chance that one of the women handing out the credentials would ask Mitch why he had sent in two fees for the night. This didn't happen and we all received our name tags. The other three guys had been very popular at school and immediately they were chopping it up with their classmates, most of whom they had not seen since 1976. Mitch, on the other hand, was being a wallflower. One thing we counted on was that since Mark, Rick and Rodney did not remember Mitch, that most others would also not remember him. I kept looking at the sign-in table to see if the real Mitch had shown up.

Following are some of Rick's memories of the night as well as his instructions to me on what to say and do in order to pull off the ruse:

There are three things I would like to add. First, the idea came from you and Mark because I remember you guys calling me up and telling me you were going to crash my reunion and you already had the idea of impersonating someone. Second, in preparation of handling someone who might say they never saw you around, you could tell them, "I was in vocational." In fact, you even used that line on Art Martinez. It was when I asked Art if he remembered you and he looked hesitant and acted like he didn't recognize you, you gave him the line about being in vocational. He seemed to accept it and moved on. Last, I remember being in a circle of guys when Steve Ponder, the only person at the reunion that actually remembered Mitch Cunningham, said he remembered you with a puzzled look on his face and that's when you replied "Well, I put on a little weight."

I do not remember many details of the night other than those offered by Rick in the above paragraph. But here's what I do recall. Most people did not remember Mitch. Several of them squinted at me and tried to see a Mitch who was ten years younger. One guy absolutely remembered Mitch and exclaimed, "Mitch! It's good to see you again." I think he even gave me a bear hug. At one point, a group of eight or ten of us stood in a circle conversing. A couple of times, Rick or Mark leaned over and whispered to me to mention a certain event like when

Johnny Jones cut off his thumb in shop class or some such thing.

The closest call of the night came later when we were circulating the room and talking to various people. One guy, Mike Curry, a tall African American guy kept looking at me and shook his head a couple of times as if he did not believe I was Mitch Cunningham. Well, he was right and he knew my name was Stan Faddis. Why? Because at the time of this reunion, I was working in Juvenile Hall. Mike, a County Social Worker, had recently been hired at the Hall as a mental health counselor and we had been introduced a month before. In that month, we had a number of talks about kids on his caseload, so he knew my real name. I quickly pulled him aside and explained what we were doing. He thought it was pretty funny and did not expose me for the fraud I was.

We successfully pulled off the stunt and, to this day, are still full of ourselves for doing so. We had a blast and now we can say we all went to our class reunion. We talk about it sometimes and let others in our our little "secret." It has been twenty-nine years since then and we never tire of rehashing it. I honestly believe that no one has a story like this one. We are the one and only.

Chapter Six

As previously stated, I worked with some staff members in Juvenile Hall who really were unnecessarily hard on the kids. These people seemed to thrive on bullying the minors and playing "King of the Mountain." One of these I will call Harry Reese. He was a big gruff man with a thick mustache who mostly growled when he spoke. He seemed to be in a perpetual bad mood with the minors. On the other hand, he did get along with some staff people and he was, at times, friendly. Reese and I did not see eye to eye on how to run a unit. Something that needs to be explained here is that there are three classifications of Group Counselors in the Hall. They are GC1, GC2 and Senior GC. At the time, I was a GC1 and he was a Senior GC because he had worked there several years longer than I. We once had a big clash in B3 where I was assigned full-time.

On one particular Sunday morning my two full-time coworkers called in sick. Reese and a part-time counselor were sent to the unit to work with me for the 7 to 3 shift. Keep in mind that this was my unit in which I worked all the time and Reese had come in to work overtime. B3 was not his assigned unit. He typically worked the 3 to 11 shift in another unit. It should also be said that sometimes Senior GC's were pulled during their shifts to work out of class as a Supervising GC. That morning, as usual, we got the kids up to go to breakfast which was just a half an hour from the time we walked in the door to begin our shift. The kids, as usual, came down to use the bathroom, wash up and comb their hair to get ready to go on the meal movement. Almost immediately Reese began barking orders at the kids whom he hardly knew because he did not work the unit. Since I knew the routine I assumed that I would take lead that day. I guess that Reese had other ideas, which I would soon discover.

The part-timer was down the hallway popping doors, I was standing at the bathroom door monitoring that area, and Reese was behind the desk. A minor went up to the desk and asked him for some hair gel which came in a tube. Reese squirted a big dollop of it onto the kid's palm and he went back into the bathroom to comb his hair. We had a standing rule that there was to be no talking in the bathroom because that is often where altercations started. The kids knew this and so they didn't talk in there. At one point, the minor who had been given the hair gel concluded he had been given too much hair gel, so without talking, he tapped his roommate on the shoulder and held out his hand for him to take some from him. The second kid did so and no words were exchanged between them. Suddenly, Reese knocked on the bathroom window and accused them of talking and advised them they would be disciplined by spending an extra hour in their room during free time. I told Reese that they had not exchanged words and had not broken any rules. He disregarded what I said and wrote their names down in the discipline log. This started what was going to quickly result in a mutiny if it was not stopped.

Reese was talking gruffly to the kids about everything; it was obvious he'd gotten up on the wrong side of the bed. I was upset because I knew how my unit would react to all this. They were sixteen-, seventeen-, and eighteen-year-old boys who were relatively mature and followed the rules. We got all the kids into set up and readied to go to breakfast. Reese decided he would structure the group and launched into a tirade. One thing he said after every kid was already seated was that he was going to go down to the rooms and every unmade bed would earn an hour of room time for those who had unmade beds. This was not a B3 rule. The kids barely had enough time to wake up, wash up and set up to go to breakfast and so we allowed them to make their beds after returning from breakfast. This announcement started the minors quietly griping, looking around at each other in disbelief, and looking to me for help. Fifty of fifty had not made their beds because they knew they were allowed to do it later.

Reese went on, evidently in an effort to cause a full-blown mutiny. He told them they could write a Grievance on him for the rules he was imposing. He went on to say, "But I'm going to be the acting supervisor on the 3 to 11 shift and I will be the one to answer your grievance which I will deny." This went over about as well as you'd expect so they grumbled and rolled their eyes at him. He had the minors stand up and get into the usual two lines to move out the door. Just as the Control Desk cleared us, he told them, "Take your combs out of your pockets and put them on your chairs." Obviously, he had just thought of this new rule and wanted to further exercise his power. This was yet another thing we did not make these kids do. They knew better than to comb their hair in line or in the cafeteria. They got even more upset. Reese was standing near the back door through which we would exit. I walked over to him and in a very low voice told him, "Sir, we don't do that in this unit." He looked at me and in a loud voice replied, "So? You're in charge of the f***ing unit now?"

He quickly opened the door and we started the movement to the cafeteria. As the unit walked into the cafeteria, Reese, who was at the head of the line, headed straight to the table where the SGC's sat. This was a table at the front of the cafeteria where two supervisors sat during meal times to monitor what was happening. There were often nearly a hundred kids in the cafeteria and it could be dangerous with all the silverware on the tables. Reese told the supervisors, "I'm sick, I'm going home and I won't be back for the swing shift either." He walked out of the cafeteria and left the premises without waiting to be relieved of duty. I had upset him by pointing out we did not run B3 the way he was trying to. It was his belief that, because he was a Senior GC and I was GC1, he was the boss. I don't think he counted on having a GC1 tell him what to do. One of the supervisors had to come back with us to the unit and take Reese's place until someone could be called in which took about an hour.

A couple of things happened as result of that incident. First, Reese was not allowed to be acting SGC for several months, something he blamed on me. The second thing was Reese and I had to meet with a supervisor for a mediation a couple of weeks later. The supervisor, Michael Smith, was a tall quiet-spoken man who was very proper in his dealings with his staff. In the meeting room he laid down the ground rules. Reese would go first and have the opportunity to air his problem with me. I was then given a chance to rebut his comments and then make my own statement about my side of the story. Reese would rebut and it would go back and forth until a resolution was reached. Reese started off by demanding I be required to apologize to him in front of the kids for making him "look bad." Remember, I approached Reese that day in a very quiet voice to tell him that this was not how we ran B3. It was not my intention to make him look bad and I only wanted to keep the unit from going off. So I said, "I will not apologize to Mr. Reese in any way, shape, or form because I did nothing wrong." That pretty much ended the mediation process. Smith advised us to work professionally together if we ever happened to be in the same unit again. The meeting was over.

A policy change resulted from this. The Procedures Manual, up until that time, did not have any rules regarding who would be in charge of the unit in the absence of the full-time Senior Counselors. So it was decided that the full-timer who was there was the one who would be in charge even if he had a lower rank than those who replaced his coworkers that particular day. This was done because whoever was the full-timer knew the program and the minors.

One night, I was working in Police Admissions on the Graveyard shift (11 p.m. to 7 a.m.) when two police officers brought in a seventeen-year-old male minor they had picked up for disorderly conduct at the San Jose Convention Center where there was a Star Trek convention being held. He had been acting strangely and in a violent way, challenging others to fight and dancing wildly. I happened to be looking out the window when they drove up and watched as one officer opened the back door to their cruiser and wrestled the minor out of the car. He was handcuffed behind his back as detainees usually are. He was so unruly that the officer had to use his baton that he threaded through the minor's bent arms in order to keep him under control as they walked to the entrance. When they got inside, it was obvious the kid was highly agitated, showing no signs of settling down. The minor was white, about 270 pounds, and stood 6'4". He had on Levi's, a long john top and wore a brown leather jacket that was scuffed up and covered with sewn on patches and writing. He wore thick-soled lace-up Doc Marten boots with his pants tucked into the tops of them. He refused to calm down even after several minutes of me trying to reason with him.

Typically, upon bringing detainees into the Hall, we asked the officers to remove the handcuffs. In this case, I asked the officer to leave him cuffed and sit him on a bench. There was no way I wanted this behemoth loose in his emotional condition. The cops asked if they could write their reports there and I said they could. They both went to sit behind the counter and began to write. The kid kept running his mouth. I called for the nurse per routine. It was required she check out new admits immediately to evaluate their mental and physical condition prior to admitting them.

Before the nurse could get there, the minor screamed out, jumped up and ran toward one of the officers. Even with his hands cuffed behind his back, he dove headfirst toward the cop, trying to go over the counter to get him. He belly-flopped onto the countertop and got stuck there. I was about eight feet away so I ran over and grabbed the kid, pulling him off the counter to a standing position. One of the officers got there to help and we danced that minor around trying to gain control. He was as strong as a bull and we were unable to get him down to the floor to contain him. The cop yelled, "Trip him!" So I did. He stumbled forward, pulling us with him. He finally fell as we approached a support column that was three by three feet square. The kid went down and his head went right through the sheet rock about a foot from the ground. It wasn't pretty, but we had him under control. We took hold of his ankles and pulled him out. As he lay there on the floor, the nurse came in. She asked him, "Do you take any medications?" The minor looked at her and said, "Yeah, and I missed them today!" No joke. Well, that settled it; the nurse refused to admit him into the Hall and the police officers had no choice but to transport him to Valley Medical Center where he was presumably placed on a 72-hour psychiatric hold. We never knew for certain because we never saw him again.

One day, I was working in Receiving (BR) on the 3 p.m. to 11 p.m. shift. Boys' Receiving was where kids were processed in and out of Juvenile Hall (JH). When a minor was admitted to JH, he was required to put all his own clothes, shoes and belongings in lockers and change into the Hall's clothes. These included underwear, brown pants with an elastic waist band, a t-shirt and slip-on deck shoes because shoelaces were not allowed. Upon being released the minors were dressed out in the clothes they had left in the locker.

Shortly before each meal, a cafeteria worker wheeled a cart containing food trays and milk into BR. These were used for feeding new admits and other kids who would be sent there for disciplinary reasons during meal times. That evening, I received a telephone call from a GC named Frank Marsh advising me he was sending a minor down to eat dinner in BR. The kid's name was Eddie Carson and at that time he was about age sixteen; he had practically been raised most of his life in Juvenile Hall. Eddie's father sold roses in downtown San Jose, peddling his wares in front of bars and restaurants. Eddie possessed zero personal hygiene habits and no desire to acquire them. This resulted in horrible body odor, greasy hair and very bad breath.

Frank told me his unit was getting ready to go on a dinner movement. The problem was that Eddie refused to shower and he stunk so badly that the kids did not want to be near him, especially in the close quarters of a double single-file line. I asked Frank how long it would be before they were to move out. He said, "About thirty minutes." I told him to send Eddie to me so I could get him showered and back to the unit in time for the meal movement. Frank said, "Stan, you don't understand. He will not shower and refuses every day to do so." I told him not to worry and to send him to me.

When Eddie entered the door, he headed straight for the food cart to get his meal. I stopped him and asked what he was doing. He said he was sent down there to eat dinner because they would not allow him to go on the meal movement. I called him over closer to me at the desk, which was right next to the bathroom. I told him to get undressed, get in the shower and clean up so that he could go back to his unit before dinner. He replied, "F**k that! I'm not going to take a shower. I don't like showering." I again told him to get in there and take a shower and he again refused. At that point I removed my shirt and laid it on the desk. Then, I unbuckled my pants and began to pull them down. Eddie, wide-eyed, asked me what I was doing. I said, "I'm going take you into the shower and make sure you clean up and I don't want to get my clothes wet." He fully believed me and within ten seconds he was stripped down and heading for the shower. Fifteen minutes later I called his unit and told them I was sending the minor back in time to make the meal movement. I assured Frank that Eddie was clean, had freshly combed hair and laundered clothes, and was fit to be around others. Frank asked me how I managed to accomplish this to which I replied, "You don't want to know." My method and the details of the incident eventually got around the Hall and I was surprised that I was never reprimanded for it. However, there is no way this stunt would be tolerated in today's Juvenile Hall. The tale is legend and still told to this day after more than twenty-five years.

In about 2005 I went to lunch with a female coworker at Togo's. As we sat outside eating, a guy came up behind and said, "Would you like to buy a rose for your lady?" I declined, saying she wasn't my lady, she was my coworker. I couldn't see him because he was behind me. I heard him shuffle off to solicit someone else. I looked in his direction when he was about one hundred feet away and couldn't believe my eyes. I hollered, "Eddie!" He turned to look at me and I called him over. I asked him if he was Eddie Carson and if he remembered me. He said he was but did not recognize me. I told him I knew him from Juvenile Hall and asked him how old he was now. He said he wasn't sure but thought he was thirty-four. I thought how sad it was that he really didn't know his age and that he had not experienced very many birthday celebrations in his life. He turned and left, in search of his next customer.

One day, B3 received two new admits. They had come in together from downtown San Jose where they had been arrested. One was a tall pimply-faced Hispanic kid who was gangly and sort of awkward whom I'll call Armando. The other one was shorter, also Hispanic and had smooth olive skin and big eyes. For the purpose of this story I will call him Robert. Their admittance slips indicated they were "D" risks, meaning there was a sexual issue. Their alleged offenses for were soliciting prostitution on the streets. Upon being dressed down in Boys' Receiving it was found that Robert was wearing girl's underwear. Due to their charges, they were not allowed to have roommates, so we put them each in a single-bed room. They were very open about their sexuality and the fact that they made money by having sex with old men. Robert was the most effeminate and he acted much like a young Latina girl. He spoke in a high, soft voice and batted his eyelashes at anyone who looked at him. He asked if people would address him by the name Roberta. It was difficult for the staff to have him in our unit because he was always flirting with the other boys and offering to have sex with them. After they were adjudicated, both Robert and Armando were released either to their parents or to a group home. I never did find out for sure.

Approximately six months later, Linda and I had some friends visit us from out-of-state. They had never been to San Francisco so we took them on a tour of the city. As we walked down the street taking in the sights and stores, I noticed a very attractive young woman dressed in a black dress talking to an elderly man. As we continued on down the street about half a block I happened to see Armando, who approached and said to me, "Well, hello Mr. Faddis. I haven't seen you in a long time!" I said hello to him and then he asked if I had seen Roberta, pointing in the direction we had come from. Suddenly, it dawned on me that I had been looking at Robert in a short black dress. I couldn't believe how much like a woman he looked. He was gorgeous, and there's no way someone could've told that he was actually a male. I asked Armando, "What are you two doing up here in San Francisco?" He responded, "What do you think we're doing? We're picking up rich old men!" Our group moved on with me shaking my head at how crazy and sad are some things in life.

Over the years, I have had a number of chance encounters like this with former residents of Juvenile Hall around Santa Clara County. The world outside the Hall is referred to as "the outs." I have probably had thirty to forty such unexpected meetings with these kids, some of whom were no longer kids by the time I saw them again. The last one I recall was as I was walking into the Probation offices and heard someone yell, "Hey, Mr. Faddis!" I looked behind me to see a man running toward me, so I stopped. When he got there he said, "Mr. Faddis, do you remember me?" He looked somewhat familiar and I said so but I didn't remember his name. I knew that since he had called me "mister" it must have been one the former residents. He told me his name and I asked him what he was doing there. He said, "I am going in to visit my son in the Hall." I asked him how old he was and he replied, "Thirty-five." He explained he was doing well now, but that his son who was fourteen was now "caught up in the life." I told him I was sorry about that and after chatting a bit we parted ways.

Every other time I have run into a former minor, with the exception of once, was like the one I described above. Each time this occurred, the person always called me "mister" and they often told me how well they were doing, that they were working, married and had children. Several of them thanked me for how I had treated them inside saying I was fair and encouraging. They often mentioned other GC's who had had a positive impact on them including Mr. Crockett, Mr. McKee and Mr. Montgomery. These three men were the ones I was most often asked about.

The exception I mentioned above happened at a Costco store in San Jose. By this time, I had been promoted to Probation Officer and had not worked in Juvenile Hall for about a year. I was shopping at the store and stopped to look at an item. While deciding to buy it or not, I got the feeling that someone was looking at me. I looked around and saw a young man of about seventeen staring at me from approximately fifteen feet away. I shrugged it off because I am so large that people stare at me; usually it's small children or the developmentally delayed. However, after a couple of minutes of this, I couldn't contain my curiosity. I walked over to him and said, "Do I know you?" He replied angrily, "F**king A you know me! You almost broke my arm in Juvenile Hall!"

Now, I admit my memory can sometimes be sketchy, but I know I had never laid hands on this kid. During my thirteen years working in the Hall, I had restrained many kids in order to break up fights or to control the ones who refused to comply with verbal commands. However, it was not usually my practice to hurt kids or put so much pressure on their joints as to cause injury. I told the minor I did not remember this and that I was certain I had never restrained him. This angered him even more because he believed I was lying and unwilling to take responsibility for it. I asked him his name, thinking that it would jar my memory, but he refused to tell me. We went back and forth for several minutes. He said, "I'm here with my big brother. I'm gonna go find him and he's gonna kick your a**!" By this time I was tired of dealing with him and I said, "Go find him. I'll be right outside the front door."

Just then, a Costco security guy approached and told us to break it up. I told him the two of us were going outside. He told us we were not going to do that and instructed me, "You go that way" pointing toward the back of the store. He told the minor to go the other way. So, I did what he said, walked down the aisle, turned the corner and headed to the exit. When I got outside, the minor was out there with his big brother who, fortunately, was less hotheaded than his sibling. I explained to him what the problem was and again denied I had harmed his little brother. I told him I had never seen the kid and that he wouldn't tell me his name. Big brother said his little brother's name was Jesus Vega. The younger one glared at me and started to say something, but his older brother told him to be quiet. He went on to say it was my word against that of Jesus and that sometimes his little brother got "mixed up" about things in his life. We parted amicably even though Jesus continued to "mad dog" me.

The following day, when I went to work, I walked from my office over to the Records area in the Hall and looked for Jesus Vega's file. Leafing through it, I discovered an Incident Report (IR), which described a restraint of Vega during a fight he had with another ward. Two things in that IR made me smile. First, I was not the one who had restrained him. Second, I had been on the scene after it was all over because I was the Acting Supervisor that day and had signed the IR after reviewing it.

Several weeks later, I happened to be in B3 to visit my friend and former coworker, Ron McKee. When I walked into the unit, McKee was sitting behind the desk so I approached, glanced quickly to my right and saw several minors in the activity area. I began talking to Ron. A minute or so later, I heard someone behind me say, "Been to Costco lately?" I turned to see Jesus Vega sitting there, locked up again. I pulled him aside with the intention of setting him straight about his mistaken identification of me. Before I could start, he said, "You know something? That day when I saw you at Costco, I was thinking about it later and I remembered it wasn't you who almost broke my arm, it was that other white guy!" I didn't bother telling him that the "other white guy" is less than half my size.

One weekday morning around 1987, while still assigned to Juvenile Hall, I reported for work at 7 a.m. as usual and walked down to my unit. I was working in B1 at the time and as I recall I had a good staff that I was able to work well with. As we began to pop doors and get the kids out for breakfast, I started feeling out of sorts and somewhat lightheaded. I advised one of my coworkers of this and he suggested that I leave the unit for a while and get a breath of fresh air. I had never felt like this before and it was somewhat alarming. I almost thought that maybe I was having a heart attack. I exited the unit and walked down to another hallway where the offices of management were located. The superintendent of Juvenile Hall, Shirley Cantu, had her office door open so I knew she was in. She saw me standing at her door and invited me in. I sat down across from her at her desk and burst into uncontrollable tears. She asked me what was wrong and through my sobbing I told her I did not know. She called down to the mental health clinic and asked for someone to come and speak with me. A few minutes later, a woman from that department came into the office and sat down. She had some questions about how I was feeling, what had caused me to cry like that, and about various other things in my life that were happening at the time. These included me worrying about my mother's medical problems, working too many hours and conflicting with my supervisor. After this short evaluation she turned to Mrs. Cantu and said, "This man needs to go to emergency psychiatric services at Kaiser right now." They had a counselor drive me there and notified my wife. It turns out I had suffered a panic attack. I admit it was one of the most frightening things I have ever been through because I couldn't explain what was going on inside me to make me lose control like that. I've always prided myself on being able to keep it together no matter what. Kaiser had them take me off work for an undetermined amount of time. They wanted to evaluate me over a few weeks to see how I was progressing.

I remember going in to pick up my first paycheck after being placed on leave. I was fine until I walked to the front of the building, but when I stepped through the main door, I felt fear pour into me and thought I was going to have another panic attack. It was like some kind of evil was pressing in on me and it scared me a lot. I got my check as quickly as possible and rushed out of there. I wondered if I would ever be able to return. From then on, I had Linda go pick up my checks.

I was off for several months and got counseling from a Kaiser therapist whom I learned was a Christian. I prayed for healing of my fear of the place. The prayer and counseling resulted in me overcoming my anxiety, and after several weeks I was released to go back. From then on, I was fine and had no other episodes of anxiety, which was such a relief. I thank God and Linda for bringing me through that dark time in my life.

This episode gave me empathy for others who suffer anxiety and helped me to be more sensitive to those who suffer from it. Prior to this, I had little regard for those with emotional challenges. It wasn't that I didn't care; I just never stopped to think about how it affected people. After going through the only time I had a panic attack, I became more aware when I detected emotional and spiritual crises in others. I adjusted my attitude and manner of talking to these folks. I tried to put myself in their shoes and gave more thought to how I could best converse with them. A big part of it (and something hard for me to do) was to stay quiet and allow the other person to talk. I believe this illustrates to them that I want them to feel free to express themselves and that I have compassion for them.

Juvenile Hall was sometimes a violent place due in part to the impulsivity and lack of restraint of the minors that resulted in chaotic events. GC's often broke up many verbal and physical altercations, some gang-related, some sexual assaults, others just because of perceived slights by one to another or just plain old personality conflicts. There were quite a few suicide attempts. I personally stopped one minor from hanging himself. During a routine room check, I found a minor with a t-shirt tied tightly around his neck, hanging from the top bunk in his room. I was able to loosen the knot and get him down. In the all the years I worked in the Hall, I can only remember one successful suicide. This is amazing in light of the many attempts that were made. I believe this was mostly due to the excellent training given to the staff as well as their vigilant awareness.

Also contributing to the problem of violence were some of the staff that seemed to enjoy agitating the kids and stirring up trouble. I worked with several GC's who were just plain mean. They treated kids unfairly and seemed to revel in the power they wielded over the population. Later, I'll speak about this bullying behavior by GC's.

I do not put myself in the same group as those GC's who were mean-spirited. In fact, I went out of my way to be nice and to be fair. This is my nature. However, sometimes it was difficult to maintain an even temper. One day early in my career I was assigned to the B1 unit that held the most serious offenders such as rapists, murderers, sexual assaultive minors, and those who had committed armed robbery. B1 also housed minors waiting to be transported to the California Youth Authority (CYA). One such minor was a kid named Randall Roman who was eighteen at the time, but had committed his offense when he was seventeen. He was white, approximately 6'3" tall and weighed about 180 pounds. I don't recall why he was being sent to CYA, other than it was a violent offense.

As I did with all the other kids, I got along pretty well with him. He was intelligent and liked the music I liked from the 60's and 70's. He could name the songs and the artists who recorded them. The thing about him was that the other minors and some of the counselors despised him. He had a sharp tongue and was always trying to get under someone's skin. I prided myself on the fact that he was unable to push my buttons and it got to the point that he stopped trying. The population of B1 at that time was typically less than twenty minors. As a result, we sometimes sat the entire unit in front of the television to watch a movie or documentary.

One day, we were setting up the minors to watch a movie complete with popcorn and soft drinks. As this was happening, Roman got into a conflict with another minor. I had seen the incident start and I knew it was Randall's fault. So, I sent him down to his room with the intention of talking to him once we had started the movie. After the other minors were settled in and the movie had begun, I told my two coworkers I was going down to Roman's room to have a talk with him. As I entered his room he was standing with his back against the right side wall. I told him what he had been doing was wrong and that I was having him sit out for a while to think about it. I went over the rules again: not causing trouble, keeping one's hands to oneself, and following instructions. I concluded by asking him if he thought he could go back down to watch the movie and behave himself. He just looked at me, totally disregarding everything I had just said. Instead, he responded, "You know Mr. Faddis, you're big and you're tough. Everyone in this place is afraid of what you could do to him if you got mad. But, do you want to know something? I know I could kick your a**."

Finally, Roman's ability to push buttons had gotten to me. Within a second, my hand went up to his neck and I pushed him against the wall, choking him. I was furious and held him there until he turned red, then purplish and then blue. Suddenly, I came to my senses and pulled my hand away. As I did so, I clearly saw my handprint on his throat that was already bruised. I was very afraid about what I had just done. To this day, I do not know what came over me. Such a thing had happened to me several times when I was younger, but I was certain those days were past.

Roman calmly said, "I want a Grievance." He was referring to a form that minors could submit when they felt their rights had been violated or they had been improperly reprimanded. Grievances covered many complaints; nearly being choked to death by a staff member was surely in that category. I knew I was in deep trouble because, not only would I lose my job, but also probably would go to go to jail for assault under the color of authority. I told Roman I would get the grievance and left to go to the desk to fetch it. My coworker asked me what was going on. I told him Roman was upset about missing the movie and he wanted to grieve it. I took the form and a pencil to the minor's room and handed it to him saying I would be back in ten minutes. I added, "If you write that grievance, the next time I grab you like that, I'm not gonna let you go." In essence I had just threatened to kill this kid. It was a stupid thing to say but I was still running on adrenaline and not thinking rationally. I was attempting to intimidate him to not write a grievance against me. I went back to the desk and tried to remain calm as I waited for the ten minutes to go by.

When I went back to his room, he handed me the form, which he had filled in completely with writing. I read it carefully; it was a perfect account of what had happened. There were no erasures or misspelled words and I knew I was going to go to jail. I handed it back to him asking if there was anything else he wanted to add. I then told him, "Randall, I really don't know what came over me. I lost my temper and I'm sorry I hurt you." A big tear appeared in the corner of that kid's eye and rolled down his cheek. He then took the grievance and tore it up into pieces. As he handed it back to me he stated, "Mr. Faddis, you are the coolest counselor in this whole f*****g place." He never said another word about the incident to me, or to anyone else I guess, and I didn't bring it up. The minor was transported to CYA about two weeks later and I never saw him again. To this day, I wonder what ever happened to Randall Roman.

One of the most fortunate things for an employee of the Santa Clara County Probation Department was that we were represented by a union--Local 1587. Being a member of 1587 meant we were paid very well, had unparalleled benefits and a generous pension. Within a couple of years of being hired, I became a union representative. At that time in my life, I was about thirty years old and although I appreciated what 1587 did for its members, I got involved in the union because I was dissatisfied with how I felt the leadership treated the Group Counselors (GC's). 1587's most prominent leaders, those in the power positions such as president, vice-president, and treasurer, were probation officers. It was my opinion that in this leadership group, GC's were second-class citizens and it was my plan to change that by getting involved. This made me a very unpopular person both to 1587's leadership as well as the management of the Probation Department. I would go with the union to meetings with Management, sit on our side of the table and bicker with Management over the issues. These were the typical things such as salaries, working conditions and personnel problems. By personnel problems I mean employees who had done unprofessional and unethical things in the course of their work. I would then go to the local meetings and bicker with them about shortchanging GC's. As I speak on this issue, I have chosen not to name names and would prefer to look at the subject as a whole.

I have always been one to fight for the underdog and I wouldn't have had it any other way. I knew going in that I would face the wrath of both sides of the table, but I didn't care. It was more important to me that everyone got a fair shake. I also believed by rocking the boat I would have a tougher time getting promoted. "So be it," I thought. Boy, was I right.

What I had against me was that I was in the minority. The others intimidated the few GC's who had voting rights on the Board and even though they agreed with me privately, they did not want to "stir the pot." They were silent at the meetings and chose to vote with those who had stronger personalities and other ideas.

I finally saw that I was at war and needed a new tactic to fight the battles. That's when I decided to become a "pamphleteer." Wikipedia offers the following definition:

> A pamphleteer is a historical term for someone who creates or distributes pamphlets. Pamphlets were used to broadcast the writer's opinions on an issue, for example, in order to get people to vote for their favorite politician or to articulate a particular political ideology. A famous pamphleteer of the American Revolutionary War was Thomas Paine with perhaps the most prestigious use of the title going to John Milton. Today a pamphleteer might communicate his missives by way of weblog, but before the advent of telecommunications, those with access to a printing press and a supply of paper used the pamphlet as a

means of mass communications outside of newspapers or full-fledged books.

I published an underground newsletter and titled it "Voices Down the Hall," in reference to the gripes and mumblings that were heard from GC's working in Juvenile Hall about labor issues. I published a total of six or seven issues over the course of the year. The newsletter utilized news-like reporting, humor and biting sarcasm that pointed out the GC's grievances. No names were used, but it was obvious who the players were. Staff loved it! 1587's leadership and Management despised it. It was printed on two sides of a letter-sized sheet of paper. I distributed it around 5 a.m. by going into the Hall through a backdoor, putting a copy in peoples' mailboxes and leaving stacks of them lying around. There was a lot of speculation as to who and how many people wrote the articles for the newsletter. I once overheard someone say that, due to the various styles in the articles, it had to have five or six authors. This cracked me up because I wrote every word of every issue. My name was thrown around as being one of the culprits but I denied it. One union rep told me many times she knew it was me who was behind it. I just smiled and told her I was hurt that she would think such a thing. I truly believe that things got better for GC's due to "Voices Down the Hall" because it brought the problems out into the open.

I paid for my "disloyalty" by not being promoted from a GC to Probation Officer for many years even though I had been eligible to promote within three years of being hired. I worked in Juvenile Hall for thirteen years before my promotion in February 1997. Many people were promoted ahead of me in spite of the fact I always scored in the top five of dozens of applicants. I tried going to the Union for support but was told it had no control over whom Management hired. I had ticked off all the wrong people and could not get a fair shake as a result. A now retired Juvenile Hall supervisor recently advised me that Management discussed me at meetings. He said I was despised and they often grumbled that they wanted to be rid of me. Because I was a good employee, was always on time and had not been disciplined for anything, they could not terminate me. Refusing to promote me was all they could do to punish me. My salvation came through two men, one I had worked side-by-side with in the Hall and one who had been my supervisor. Mike Mathiasen was the coworker. He knew my work ethic and potential. During the hiring process, he said he believed I would be a good Probation Officer (PO) saying, "I would want Stan on my team if I had the choice." The other man was Harold Maclean whom I had worked under in the Electronic Monitoring Program. By this time, he was a Manager and agreed with Mathiasen, and so I was allowed through the "pearly gates." I should admit that by the time I was finally promoted, I had laid low for a number of years, not stirring the pot and just keeping my mouth shut. Later in my career, when I was held back from being promoted to a supervisory position, I published an anonymous blog named "The Probation Guy" in which I satirized Management and criticized their leadership.

At the time I was writing the newsletter, and later when I had the blog, I knew it was not a Christian thing to do, but I didn't care. I was hurt and my ego was bruised so I lashed out in the most hurtful way I could think of. I used my sarcasm and humor to exact revenge on those who were holding me back. On the other hand, I am not sorry for standing up to Local 1587 and Management, but I should have done it openly, without the subterfuge. I knew then that I was going to be punished for opposing these two entities, but I refused to keep my mouth shut. In retrospect, I should have left it at that and not been mean through the use of the newsletter and the blog. I now regret my actions and I hope those I have wronged would forgive me.

Some of the people I worked with had problems of their own and sometimes brought those things into work. At times, they allowed their personal baggage to spill out on the job resulting in them being unfair, snapping at the wards, unnecessarily disciplining them, and putting hands on a kid when it wasn't warranted. Some of these GC's were tough to work with because they treated their fellow workers badly. More than once I admonished these people to stop taking their problems out on the kids or the other staff. Some took it well and even apologized for their behavior. A couple of them responded much less graciously. Being an "enforcer" like that caused me to pay attention to my behavior and kept me in check. I can now see how God used these situations to move me closer to being the man He wants me to be. I see now that I answer to the most Supreme Being in the millions of universes of which He is the creator. Such a thought overwhelms and humbles me.

Working in probation was a good fit for me but it took quite a few years for me to realize it. In college, I found out I was good with people and figured that being a youth pastor best suited me. However, God put me on a different path on which I was allowed to use my life experiences, skills and talents in a broader way. Working with churched kids is pretty easy compared to kids who are not churched. Both groups have kids who face challenges but it seems to me now that those who go to church have positive role models. Most all the young people who get caught up in the juvenile offender system are from broken homes, most of which are headed by the family's mothers. This is not to say that such homes are not good, just not the ideal type. I come from such a home and the fact I had no male who was there all the time definitely made things harder for my mom and me. I developed a great respect for mothers who are in this position and as a probation officer did my best to help out. I often thank God for giving me the career I had. I tell people that being a probation officer is an honorable vocation. It allowed me to help those who wanted help and also fulfilled my need to hold offenders accountable.

Chapter Seven

Simply stated--I am a blessed man. I could not have dreamed a better family and life than the one God has gifted me. I admit I am more cognizant of this than when I was in my twenties and thirties. I was a much more self-centered and arrogant man during those years. I truly do not deserve the wife and children I have. Yes, I provided for them financially, but fell far short of being the emotional and spiritual leader I could and should have been. I was prideful and ignorant. It was mostly all about me, and I do not like that guy. However, I think I have recovered from my "stupid phase" and am doing my best to make up for it. I have a beautiful wife who loves God with all her heart and loves me, too. My children, when they were small, adored me and almost always ran to see me when I came home from work. They squealed with delight, hugged me and poured out their love to me, which made me proud and happy. As they got older, we went through the usual conflicts about freedom, their friends and some of the choices they made, but in spite of it all, they still loved me.

Because Linda stayed home with our children, she did a lot more activities with them, such as going on nature walks in the neighborhood, to the library, dance recitals, tae kwon do lessons, AWANAS, and soccer. For several years Heather and Holly were involved in the San Jose Children's Musical Theater, which was a lot of fun for us. We also went to Disneyland, Universal Studios and house boating on Shasta Lake. God also blessed us in another way in that our kids have all been healthy. Like I said, I am blessed. This reminds me that none of us deserve being so richly blessed by the Lord. However, we can show Him our gratitude by being obedient to Him.

By 1990, Daniel was sex, Heather was five, and Holly was three; I had been working for Probation for almost six years. Linda and I discussed getting out of the apartments. We didn't want to raise our children in the city, especially in an apartment building where their only play area was a cement driveway and parking spaces. By then, many of the SJBC students had left and the tenants were not the best. Some were just downright trouble. One night I was watching TV around 10 p.m. and heard a commotion just outside our front door that I quickly surmised was a fight. I opened the door and a woman was standing there watching several men fighting. She had an infant in her arms and was trying to stop the fight, which involved her boyfriend. I couldn't believe she was putting her baby in harm's way. I grabbed the little girl from the woman, took her inside the apartment and called 9-1-1. The next day I went out to look at the damage. There were several broken beer bottles on the driveway. Right then I decided we were going to get out of there--free rent or no free rent.

A few days later, I heard Linda on the phone in our bedroom talking to her friend, Sue Renfro, about the Christian preschool Sue was founding in Winters, California where she was currently living. The gist of the conversation was that Sue still needed another teacher. I walked into the room and gave Linda the "time out" sign. I told her to let Sue know we would be moving to Winters. I had no plan how it would work out, but God did. Within a few weeks Linda and the kids were living with Sue, her husband Chris, and their children. I stayed in San Jose for a few months until I found a new apartment manager and went to Winters on my weekends.

We looked for a house to rent, while living with the Renfros for about three months. We found a very nice, large house on fifty acres of walnuts that was perfect for us. I know

God's hand was on us in this because there were two other families who also wanted to rent it, but the owner, Mr. Knabke, chose us. The four years we lived in Winters were very good for our family. It was a town of about 9,000 residents so our children were able to experience not only living in a small town, but also growing up in the country. Linda and I both came from small towns and it was good to have given the same experience to the kids. There was plenty of room for them to run and play. Sometimes Linda turned on the hose and make a big mud puddle for them to play in. We had dogs and grew a garden with tomatoes, peppers and corn among other things. Our children played on soccer teams and took tae kwon do classes. To this day, they talk about how much they loved the tire swing their Grandpa Reed hung in a huge tree in the backyard. As adults, they have gone back to see the house on Boyce Road. Reportedly, their tire swing is still there.

Although our time in Winters, California was wonderful, the hundred-mile commute each way to San Jose for me to work began to wear me out. Finally, we had to move back to the city but even that turned out to be a blessing. We were able to rent a house in Willow Glen from Mr. Mannina, the man for whom we formerly managed the 781 apartments. He generously rented us the house in the most expensive zip code in San Jose for a very low sum and kept it there for the entire sixteen years we resided in it.

Daniel was our first-born and only son. Linda and I were full of pride and love for him. As a father, I was proud of my macho self for fathering a son even though I know I had nothing to do with the chromosomal process. One of my favorite images is Daniel wearing only his beloved cowboy boots and a swimming suit; no shirt. I nicknamed him

"Rooster" because he woke us up each day at the crack of dawn. When Daniel was five we agonized about sending him to Kindergarten in a public school because we didn't want him to learn bad things from the other kids. The first day after school he told me, "Dad, I know what the "F" word is." My heart sank as our worst fears were confirmed. However, my devious side wanted to hear him repeat it so I asked him to say it. He said, "Fart." Talk about relief! I laughed and told him, "Yes, son, that is the F word, so don't say it."

Daniel accepted Christ at age ten and I baptized him and his sister Heather in a friend's swimming pool. He was raised in a Christian environment, was home-schooled until high school when we sent him to Valley Christian School. I will say more about him later in this book.

On August 3, 1985, our oldest daughter, Heather Lea Faddis came into the world. She was a happy little girl who liked to dress up in her mom's dresses, shoes and play house with her sister, Holly. Her blond hair and huge blue eyes reminded me of Precious Moments figurines. Unfortunately, I do not have a lot of specific memories of her upbringing due to hardly being home and my neglecting to pay a lot of attention to my children during those years.

Heather had a number of boys who liked her, most of whom I did not approve. We butted heads because I couldn't keep my mouth shut, telling her she could do better. Like so many girls I've known, she was attracted to boys (and they were boys, not men) whom I believed were not in her league. When she was nineteen years old, she talked about moving to Austin, Texas with her girlfriend to take advantage of the growing job market there. I was all for it, primarily because I thought that meant her getting away from her boyfriend, Adam. I told her so. Then she advised me that Adam was going with them and my heart sank. I was sitting in my recliner as we talked and, at that point, I patted my leg, signaling her to sit on my lap. I told her I didn't want that because I worried she would miss her family so badly that in her loneliness she would end up having sex with Adam. I had given her a purity ring a couple of years prior and I was certain she had honored her vow of chastity, to wait until she was married. At that moment, her big blue eyes filled with tears and in a whisper she said, "Daddy, I'm pregnant."

Her revelation hit me like a train; it filled me with sadness and anger at the same time. In my mind, she had ruined her life and would never fulfill the dreams I had for her. Heather could have been a doctor, a lawyer or anything she wanted to be but now, being saddled with a baby, none of those dreams would come to be. As we talked further, I asked her if it had been her plan to go to Austin to have the baby and give it up for adoption before Linda and I could find out, and she acknowledged that it was so. Strangely, this made it easier for me. I figured once the baby was born and adopted out, she could go ahead with her life unencumbered.

The plan to move to Austin never happened but Heather began to look for a couple who wanted to be parents but were unable to have children of their own. She settled on one, but deep in my gut I believed she would not follow through which, of course, was her prerogative. When Luca was born, she decided not to give him up. I saw that the second I watched her holding that little man, lying there in a hospital bed. A little over a year later she got pregnant by Adam again and they decided to get married which they did a couple of weeks after Logan was born. Eventually, Heather and Adam divorced and she is married now to Sam who is the father of their three beautiful girls, Cambria, Caedence and Quinn. She is a great mother and I adore those five grandchildren. They bring me so much joy and laughter and all love their grandpa.

Heather has some interesting avocations including that she is a doula, assisting pregnant women through their pregnancies. She desires also to be a mid-wife. Her two youngest daughters were born at home. She is also very knowledgeable regarding homeopathic medicine and treating illnesses with herbs. Heather has a soft spot for the homeless and the down-and-out. Often, she takes food to people she sees on the street. Oh, and she is enamored with giraffes.

Our daughter, Holly, was born while I was gallivanting in Tahiti. I was there exploring the possibility of starting a travel business with my college friend Gary Williams. Linda and I thought it wouldn't be a problem for me to go on that trip, as Holly was not due for another six weeks. I was expecting Linda to meet me at SFO but quickly learned that Holly had to be delivered by C-section and they were in the hospital. Linda has AB negative blood, which unexpectedly attacked Holly's white blood cells requiring the emergency delivery.

Holly spent the first thirty days of her life in the intensive care nursery because she weighed four pounds. It was a scary thing to go through but we were sure the Kaiser nursery was the best place she could have been, reportedly even better than Stanford. Linda had toxemia and was not allowed to hold Holly but was able to express milk that I was able to feed her with a bottle. I had some very tender moments with her as I fed her several times. Linda spent about six days in the hospital and then we went twice a day to visit Holly until she was released. The single word I have to describe Holly is "joyful." She is fun to be with and her kindness is immense.

Like Heather, Holly had several boyfriends who were not up to my standards. They were nice enough but not the types I wanted to be the father of my grandchildren. As a dad, I reserve that right. I sometimes have to remind myself that I was not up to the standards my in-laws, Reed and Peggy Shackelford, had for their daughter's husband. But now, after thirty-five years, I believe I have shown them I am a good husband to Linda and a good father to their grandkids. Holly is now married to Bryan and they have two sons, Judah and Joshua. Of course, the love the boys and I have for one another is mutual.

When I wrote about my sister, Tina, I mentioned she gave birth to two children. The youngest is a boy whose name is Derrick. Tina had him when she was in prison at the California Rehabilitation Center (CRC) in Norco, CA. I recollect that he was two days old when CPS took him to live with his foster mother. He has remained with her since then. I have only seen him a few times. He lives twenty miles from me but doesn't seem to be interested in having a relationship with me. I don't blame him and I hope we will reconnect someday.

Tina's oldest child is Meagan Nicole Faddis. She is now in her mid-twenties, and has quite a backstory. As I have said, Tina was a heroin addict. She believed, due to her drug abuse, she was sterile and unable to have children. She was five-and-a-half months pregnant with Meagan and using heroin daily when she discovered she was carrying a child. She was given Methadone that she took daily. So, when Meagan was born she was addicted to Methadone and spent the first month of her life in an intensive care nursery while they weaned her off the drug.

Tina initially went to prison for several years. The doors to that place were like those revolving doors in a department store for her. Meagan was six months old when she first came to live with us when Tina went back to prison on a parole violation. We did not have legal custody of Meagan so every time Tina violated (by submitting positive drug tests to her parole agent) and was sent back to CDC, we took Meagan in, but once Tina was released, she would take her back. This occurred a number of times between the ages of six months and five years of age. Meagan went to a foster home for a couple of years when Tina lost custody of her.

When she was eight, the Court in Stanislaus County held a custody hearing at which it was discussed what was to be done with Meagan. Tina was again in custody at this time and Meagan was in a new foster home because she had allegedly attacked her foster mother with a bicycle chain and the woman took her to the police station and dropped her there. I went to the hearing; her family law attorney advised me that Meagan was going to be put up for adoption due to Tina's numerous failures to reunify with her per the Court's order. Tina's addiction was stronger than her desire to be a good mother. I went to a public phone to call Linda to advise her of this. Linda immediately said we could not let it happen and we should take Meagan into our home.

I went into the courtroom when the bailiff called the case and watched as my sister was escorted in wearing a jail jumpsuit and shackles. At some point, I stood and asked permission to speak, asking that the Court consider granting custody to Linda and me. The judge asked me what our occupations were. I said Linda was a schoolteacher and I was a probation officer. Custody was instantly granted to us.

Meagan lived with us on and off. She is now twenty-four. When she was between the ages of eight and eleven, I took her numerous times to see her mother when she was housed at the Northern California Women's Facility (NCWF) in Stockton, CA. It was a chore but I wanted them to have time together because I had hope that Tina would straighten out and be able to get Meagan back. We visited on Saturdays for three or four hours. After processing, all the visitors walked to a large day room that contained small round tables with several chairs around them. The room had many windows in order to make it as bright and sunny as possible. I always took twenty dollars in one-dollar bills and quarters for the vending machines. Tina liked the cheeseburgers and Meagan liked the microwave popcorn. We spent the time talking and playing board games or cards. Sometimes, Meagan played with the children of the other inmates. I really don't know if Meagan enjoyed these visits or not. I believe she had a lot of anger toward her mom whom she felt had abandoned her. If so, I share the same animosity with her, but I never spoke badly of Tina to Meagan during that time in her life. She already had enough to deal with.

Two or three times Meagan and I went to NCWF for "family visits" which lasted for two nights and almost three days. We took our own food in an ice chest and paper bags. After we and our possessions were searched, a correctional officer took us to a duplex that sat next to the prison and inside the fifteen-foot-tall fence. The unit had two bedrooms, a living room, kitchen and bathroom. It was as comfortable as they could make it, I suppose, but it still had the look of an institution. From the small lawn outside, I could see my car parked in the lot about one hundred yards away; close but not obtainable. My thought was that this was what the prisoners experienced when they looked out and could see the free world that lay just beyond that fence.

Meagan's relationship with Linda and me has been rocky at times. For the most part, we have gotten along, but other times, not so much, just like with the other children. Even though we are Meagan's aunt and uncle we took her into our family and gave her everything we had given our biological children.

In spite of her past problems, Meagan has a lot to offer. She is very smart, pretty and has a great personality. I enjoy watching her interact with Heather's and Holly's children. As I was writing this, I remembered something I use to do to Tina in the grocery store when we were teenagers. When we were well into the store, I would take something off the shelf and tell her in a loud voice in the manner of a child, "Mommy, can I have this? Please, mom, please!" Or, I would say very loudly, "Mom, I have to go to the bathroom!" These antics caused Tina much embarrassment and it mortified her. She gritted her teeth and hissed for me to "Stop it!" This, of course, made me do it all the more and Tina would head straight to the exit. Well, when Meagan was a teenager, I did it to her, too. She appreciated it about as much as her mother did.

My hope for all three of my girls, is that they will be as close to God as possible, see how precious they are in my eyes and find happiness in life.

I recently watched the movie *Chasing Mavericks*. It's a true story about a young surfer from Santa Cruz, Jay Moriarity. It's a very good movie and is family friendly. If you get it (I rented it from Red Box), watch it in Blu-Ray if you have a Blu-Ray player. It is a visually stunning movie and illustrates the power and majesty of the ocean.

Watching this movie made me recall my own experience with the Pacific Ocean, which taught me how small and weak I am in a quite painful way. In May 2000, our family flew to Maui for an eleven-day vacation. We stayed in a great hotel in Kehei called the Mauna Kai. We had lots of fun doing the typical stuff like snorkeling, sightseeing and going to a luau. I have my motorcycle license so I rented a Harley Road King and everyone took turns riding with me around the island. Five members of my family (Linda, Daniel, Heather, Holly and Meagan) were able to bask in the sun and sand for the entire eleven days. I, on the other hand, participated in the vacation for a lesser amount of time.

On our fifth day, we discovered a small piece of heaven called Big Beach. The six of us arrived at Big Beach, south of Kihei, in our rented mini-van and unloaded our beach gear, which included several boogie boards. As we traipsed through the trees on a path that took us down to the water, none of us noticed the posted signs that read, "Caution!" "Swim at your own risk!" "No lifeguard on duty." I guess the beautiful white sand and azure water distracted us. The ocean was so inviting and the waves were just the right size for us. We estimated them to be three or four feet high. As soon as we hit the beach, Heather, Daniel and I grabbed one of the three boards and headed for the water. We were spread out about thirty or so yards apart.

Linda, Meagan, and Holly sat on the beach and watched us. As I have written before, I love salt water and being as fat as I am, I float like a cork. The snorkeling I have done in Tahiti and the Caribbean was fun and I am very comfortable in the ocean, or at least I was until that fateful day on Maui. Things were going well, that is, until they went wrong. After taking several waves and riding them all the way onto the beach, I headed out again for another one. I suddenly realized the next approaching wave was much bigger than the previous ones. It must have been eight or nine feet and it scared me! I tried to swim to the beach but the undertow was too strong for me to make it. So, I turned back to the ocean and dove into the wave like I was supposed to, but I was a second too late. The wave broke just as I dove toward it and it picked me up and had its way with me. I went limp and tried to ride it out. I don't know how long I was underwater but I didn't panic and I just knew it would gently deposit me onto the beach. But it was not to be.

Suddenly, the angry, crashing waves slammed me into the beach. I landed on the back of my head and the weight of that water folded me in half. In spite of my huge belly, my knee hit me in the forehead. Talk about compression. I crawled further up the beach trying to get away from the water. I was whispering something like, "I'm hurt! I'm hurt real bad." I was unable to speak louder than that. I heard Holly and Meagan tell Linda, who was videotaping the action, that Dad was hurt and needed help. Linda's response: "He's just kidding. He's not hurt." The pain in my side was terrible and it was difficult to breathe. I struggled to get up to my feet, but the second I did, another wave knocked me down again. I got up again to walk the rest of the way up onto dry land at which time I noticed my shorts had been ripped off me and I was as bare as a tree in winter, out there for everyone within a hundred yards to see. The kids tried to shield my nakedness by standing the boogie boards on the ends, creating a wall of sorts. I sat down and Linda covered me with a towel, still filming the action (just kidding).

An off-duty lifeguard from another beach happened to be there, enjoying the afternoon. He ran over to us to do triage on me. He had his radio with him so he summoned help. The kids were crying and I was hurting like never before or since. A bit later some big, strong Hawaiian firemen walked up in response to the call for help. They were carrying a backboard that was all of eighteen inches wide. I am a good thirty inches wide and there is no way I could lay on that thing. I looked up at the firemen and said, "I weigh over four hundred pounds and I'll stand up and walk off this beach before I'll make you guys carry me off." One of them said, with a look of relief on his face, "Thank you, brother!" The lifeguard partially deflated the tires on his pick-up and drove it from the road to where we were. They helped me get up and sit on the tailgate and we slowly drove out to the road where an ambulance was waiting. By that time the adrenaline was wearing off and the pain in my side was beyond description. On top of that, I could hardly breathe. Doing so made it hurt even more and my left side felt like it was stuffed with burning cotton. The hospital was more than twenty miles away on winding, bumpy roads. It was obvious the driver knew the location of each pothole on that road because she hit every one of them. I thought I was going to pass out. This would have been a relief, but I had no such luck. The EMT riding in back with me said I was fortunate because I had not broken my neck. He speculated this was due to my substantial girth. He went on to relate that he had personally taken two men off that beach whose tangle with the waves resulted in them now being quadriplegics. He also advised me that Big Beach was one of the most dangerous on the island, which is why there were no lifeguards there. The municipality of Kihei did not want to be sued for any injuries people suffered, thus the warning signs to not swim there and no lifeguards. On top of that, he said the summer swell had come in the day prior, which caused the huge rogue wave that hit me.

At the ER, X-rays showed I had fractured six ribs and punctured my left lung. The attending doctor said it was more accurate to say my ribs were "shattered." I was admitted to the hospital. Well, so much for my dream vacation in the sun. Linda and the kids didn't want to leave me alone in the hospital and said they would stay with me. God bless them, but no way was I going to allow that so I insisted they could visit me each day for a short time after which they had to go and do vacation types of things. They did so, reluctantly.

Most of my caregivers were small Filipino women who were kind and attentive. Their cheery demeanor was one thing that kept me going. The other thing was Demerol administered intravenously. It is said that childbirth is the most intense pain that women ever endure. I cannot argue with that due to the obvious reason. However, I nominate fractured ribs as second most painful. The nurses instructed me that when the pain became too intense, I was to summon them and they would bring Demerol. I usually held out as long as I could until it hurt so much I nearly cried. Almost immediately after I would hit the "call button" and ask for some pain relief, the nurse would bring in a syringe and put it into my IV. A few seconds later, I would feel warmth, starting at the top of my head and travelling down to my toes, and the pain disappeared. This experience helped me to somewhat understand why heroin users become addicts. After the drug was administered, I was euphoric and probably wouldn't have cared if someone had punched me in the side at that moment.

I was still in the hospital when our vacation ended, but I was not well enough to go home, so my family left without me. My nurses continued to tenderly care for me and make my stay as nice as it could be. Two friends from our college days lived on the island so they visited me a few times. Even the couple that owned the Harley rental shop came to see me.

I was in that hospital for a total of thirteen days. I would often tell my nurses how much I appreciated them and was as polite as I could be. I didn't complain at all because they were so lovely and kind. I was embarrassed that they had to perform certain duties to care for my "hygienic needs" and I told them so. They just smiled and told me it was okay and they didn't mind doing it. I loved their singsong voices and smiles. Once the word got out that I was going to be discharged, several of them came to say good-bye and some told me I was the best patient they ever had.

Even though I have traveled quite a bit, I had never bought travel insurance. However, for this trip I did, and it was the best money I have ever spent. The insurance paid for Linda to fly back to Maui to accompany me home and covered the cost of her hotel for two additional days while waiting for me to get discharged. Of course, the six of us had flown there in coach, but the doctor said I wouldn't be able to handle that for the trip back. He called the insurance company about it and they sent us home in First Class, all on their dime. That was the only time I had ever been in the First Class section. I only wish I could have enjoyed it. The pain in my side was still severe and I know I would have hardly survived coach class.

To this day, I have not gone back into the ocean, and watching surfers on TV or movies such as *Castaway* give me the shivers. My snorkeling and boogie boarding days are over. I'm not one "to get back up that horse."

Chapter Eight

For seven years I taught vocational training to probation officers and juvenile hall counselors. I would often begin my presentation on the first day saying that who we are as people is shaped greatly by our upbringing. And, that how we treat those in our charge is often determined by our own upbringing. I have since added to this that our closest friends also have a huge impact on who we eventually become; sometimes our associates shape us more than our families do.

If we associate primarily with people of low morals and poor behavior we risk falling into those same patterns. How many times have we seen "good" kids from loving homes fall into the "wrong" crowd and end up in sad circumstances? I don't have to look farther than my own family to see this pattern. All three of my siblings were drug and alcohol users in spite of our mother's loving and stable care. All three of them came to associate with people of low character and bad habits. All three of them died while driving under the influence of alcohol or methamphetamine. As of the time I was teaching, only one of my siblings (my brother Kevin) had died in a solo car crash while driving drunk. His friend was with him but he survived only to die later in life by overdosing on methamphetamine. In trying to make the point above about how our associations shape us, I told my students about Kevin. Every time, someone would ask, "How is it that you didn't turn out the same way"? My answer was and still is that it is due to the fact that I chose to become a Christian as a teenager and I do my best to follow the teachings of the Bible. I have said many times before that if it were not for having Jesus in my life, I would either be sitting on a barstool or living in a prison cell, or I'd be dead.

My belief in God is what has saved me from an early death and has guaranteed me eternal life in heaven. I believe that He has a plan for me and I want to serve Him as much and as long as I can. This plan included me being the first person in my family to go to college. As I have said, my father had seven brothers. My Dad and several of his brothers did time in jail or prison. They were tough and violent men and I did not want to be like that.

Now, let me get to my main point... Several guys I met in college in the late 1970's remain my friends to this day, nearly forty years later. They have impacted my life in such a positive way and stuck by me all these years. To me, this is one of the most precious things about going to San Jose Bible College. It was small and intimate. Of course, at age nineteen and into my twenties I didn't think about remaining friends with anyone for the next thirty-eight years and counting. When you're young, such things don't cross your mind because you only live in the moment. But, at fifty-eight I am blessed to count as my closest friends (in alphabetical order, not chronologically or ranking of importance) Dave Baker, Darren Briggs, Rick Criscione, Bill Dobos, Wayne Ford, Mike Huskey, Dennis McGuire, Brad Pitt (just kidding), Mark Thompson, and Lowell Weare, among others. I have more friends than these but they are not as close as those mentioned above. I have talked to men who tell me they have few or no friends and that breaks my heart as well as makes me even more grateful for the ones I have.

Of those mentioned above, Dennis McGuire is the one I have known the longest. We met a few days before school started at freshman orientation. We have been friends through thick and thin and he is like a brother to me. One of my favorite memories is that Dennis wore his hair long in high school and right up to the day before he arrived at college. I believe that at some point it was nearly down to his waist. But the school rules included that young men were to have short hair, so the day prior to coming to SJBC, Dennis had his locks cut off. It aggravated him that upon his arrival, there were several upperclassmen who had long hair. I laughed when I heard his story.

Dennis and I, along with others including Kevin Troutt, Dave Jacobs and Linda Avrit were later the leaders in a ministry to high school students called Mansion. The ministry had been started years before by a previous group of students. It met on Saturday nights and consisted of worship music, a skit by the staff that we made up just the hour before the program started, and a teaching time by one of the leaders. It was called "Mansion" because when it was founded, the weekly meeting was held in the old Hayes Mansion in San Jose near Frontier Village Amusement park which is now gone. However, the Mansion has since been remodeled and turned into a beautiful hotel; it is still in use.

Whenever I consider those of my friends who have influenced me the most in spiritual things, I think of Lowell and April Weare. Linda and I got to know the Weares somewhat by accident but, as I look back on it, I now realize God must have strategically placed them into our lives.

Lowell was a fellow student at SJBC. One semester short of his graduation, he decided to quit and the Weares moved back to Sandy, Oregon from where they had come. I don't really know the circumstances of this and it's not relevant to my story. We did not know the Weares very well at that time.

The following year we were managing the apartments at 781 S. 11th. St. and I got a call from Lowell. He said they were planning to come back to San Jose for him to finish his last semester and they needed an apartment to live in with their two-year-old daughter, Leah. I told him we had no vacancies; however, after discussing it with Linda, I called Lowell back and said they were welcome to live with us for that final semester of school if they wanted to. This was prior to us having our own children and we had a two-bedroom apartment. A short time later the Weares moved in with us. Offering our home to them for that four months was one of the greatest blessings of our lives because we got to know Lowell and April so well and were able to see Jesus through them in a way we had never experienced before.

While the Weares lived with us, we had many meals together. Their two-year-old daughter, Leah, sat next to me at the dinner table. It is our custom to all hold hands as someone said grace before eating. However, Leah didn't want to hold my hand so she would only grasp my pinkie finger between her thumb and forefinger each time we prayed. It was funny and cute and we still laugh about it to this day. Leah is now married to a man named Tom Payne. She has a Ph.D. from Vanderbilt University and her dad gets a kick out of calling her Dr. Payne.

The Weares are two of the most godly people we have ever had the pleasure of knowing. The way that they model Jesus has taught us much. Linda and I appreciate them and love them deeply because of it. I hope that every couple could have a Lowell and April Weare in their lives.

I was part of a group of guys that call ourselves "The Dudes." We all got to know one another at San Jose Bible College, and even though we've sometimes not had much contact over the years, we have remained friends and still get together when we have the chance.

Back in the late 70's I met a young man like myself who eventually came to be my best male friend. I say "late 70's" because I only recall it was 1977 or 1978. You'll have to excuse me for not recalling certain details of events that occurred over thirty-five years ago. I specify "male friend" because as a married man, I am required by political correctness and in the interest of my own well-being to profess that my best friend is my wife, Linda, who has been chained to me for over thirty-five years and has done a stellar job at it, I might add.

At any rate, Bill Dobos and I became friends when we met at San Jose Bible College. He came to the school from Southern California. Bill entered into our circle of friends which included Rick Criscione, George Gardner, Mike Huskey, Dennis McGuire and Mark Thompson. (Please note that the preceding names are in alphabetical order so there can be no argument about any particular guy's importance or lack thereof).

Because I did not have wealthy parents to pay my tuition, my game plan for college was to attend classes for a semester and then work a semester to earn money for tuition for the next one. This is partly why I started college in November 1976 and graduated with my B.S. (yes, I get comments from my friends that having a B.S. is so fitting for me) in May 1984. My grades were not the best and I graduated Barely Made It Laude. To be very honest I was not a model student. I skipped a lot of classes; I had poor (non-existent) study habits; and I was more about having fun than anything else. Now, had SJBC offered a Bachelor's Degree in Good Times, I might have been elected the valedictorian of my class.

To further express the truth, Linda and I got married in 1980 and she worked full time so that I didn't have to (we did manage an apartment building and got free rent) and so she put me through school my last three years. This sort of illustrates the "being chained to me" part as mentioned above.

Due to my intermittent enrollment, Bill and I had sporadic contact. He got married the year after I did and we graduated in 1984. We had a few adventures with a couple of guys in our circle; however, I am not at liberty to divulge those escapades until our attorneys have properly advised us. I will say that one of them involved Bill failing to STAY IN THE CAR as he was instructed. At one point in time, Bill and his wife Janean managed the apartments at 780 South 11th Street and Linda and I were the managers across the street at the 781's. We lost contact once we each moved away from there and only talked on the telephone two or three times a year.

Around 1988, Bill was called to pastor a small church in Weston, Oregon, a tiny town in the far northwest part of the state. A search of Google showed that Weston's population in 2010 was 670 (people). Bill has served that community for over twenty-five years and he has done a tremendous work there. He has the heart of an elephant. He is the most well-read person I know (which I attribute somewhat to the fact that there is nothing else to do in Weston). A couple of times over the years, Bill and his family came to visit us in San Jose. Linda and I visited them in Weston a couple of times.

Bill truly cares about folks and he is generous even though he did not get rich by accepting the pastor position in Weston. Shortly after the Dobos family moved to Weston I went to visit them. This particular time I was by myself. During my visit, Bill noted that my car tires were pretty worn and he thought they should be replaced soon. I blew it off saying they had lots of miles left on them. The next day as I was leaving for home, Bill handed me a plain envelope and made me promise not to open it until I was many miles away. I said OK and drove off. I stopped just past the city limit and looked inside the envelope where I found $300 and a note instructing me to get some better tires.

In 2009, a few months before Bill turned fifty, Janean sent us an invitation to attend a surprise party for him in Weston. She asked the invitees to write something for Bill that would be read at the party. I did not plan to go due to the distance so I wrote my take on Bill and mailed it to her with my regrets that I couldn't be there. A few days before the party, I decided to go. Linda was unable to tag along so I drove up to Weston by myself. I did not tell Janean I was coming. I stayed in a motel the night before and walked into the venue (the Weston Community Center) unannounced. I was able to surprise those who know me including Janean, her children and several old friends from our college days. Bill was shocked to see all these people who had come to his surprise party. Janean had pulled it off without a hitch. At the appointed time, I was asked if I would read what I had written to Bill. I did, but not without a few tears. It was an honor to be there and many of the people had things to say about him which reinforces what I have written here about Pastor Dobos.

On June 21, 2012, when I called Bill to tell him that our son Daniel had committed suicide he immediately said he and Janean would be coming down to Turlock to support us. I did not expect this but it didn't surprise either me because, as I've said, he has the heart of an elephant. It is no easy task for him to leave his town and the people there because he is such an integral part of his community. People rely on him for moral support, friendship and many other things. Bill is a servant and when we get to heaven he'll visit me in my thatched roof hut and I'll go see him in the palatial mansion that I know God is building for him. He's a soft-spoken and deeply thoughtful man whose gentleness and wisdom are greatly needed and appreciated. I am speaking from my own personal experience. We have spent many hours on the telephone; him counseling me through whatever rough patch I was going through at that moment.

I later called him back and said, "Well, since you're already coming, would you mind doing Daniel's memorial for us?" He said he would and I knew it would be a great service. Over the next couple of days we talked by telephone a few times. He gave me a thumbnail sketch of how he planned to handle the service. He mentioned he had done several services of those who have taken their own lives. I also found out from his wife, Janean, that although their town and the church's congregation are small, Bill is asked by many people in the area for help when they are grieving and he has officiated dozens of funerals. He is sometimes on the scene when people pass into the hereafter and has assisted funeral directors removing bodies from homes, many of whom were his friends. To me, this is far and beyond the call of duty and when I have told Bill how much I respect him for the ministry he has, he just shakes it off. I have never met a more humble person than Bill Dobos. He loves God. He loves his family and his friends. And he loves his fellow man.

Bill and Janean arrived here the Wednesday before Daniel's service on Saturday. On Friday, he asked to meet with our family as well as Daniel's fiancée Michelle and her parents, Joe and Debbie. We all spent an hour in our living room talking about the service. Bill asked each of us if there was something special we wanted him to mention. He asked us to tell him about what we liked about Daniel. He said if anyone wanted to they could either speak at the service or write something he could read for them. He encouraged us that if we did want to speak, to write down what we would say so that in the event we could not make it through, he could finish reading the remembrance. He was a comforting presence to all of us and I hope if you ever have to go through an experience like this, you will find your own Bill Dobos to help you through it.

One evening a couple of days after the service, we were sitting in my living room talking. At one point, Bill told me, "Stan, you are my best friend." In all my years of life I had never heard these words. I was overwhelmed and I began to cry because it touched my heart so deeply. I have a few other guys who have called me a "good friend" or ONE of their best friends, but never has anyone called me "THE best." Bill explained that our friendship is so precious to him, citing most of what I have recounted here. He said it meant so much that I drove all that way to help him celebrate turning fifty and he felt it cemented me into that special role as his best friend.

As I got ready to post this entry to my blog, I realized that somewhere on my hard drive could be found my birthday letter to Bill. I located it and even though some of it is redundant to the above, I feel compelled to add it here:

I have known Bill Dobos since the late 1970's. We met at San Jose Bible College when we were yet young men. Now, in our fifties, we are still friends and I appreciate that so much.

Although we have had little face-to-face contact since we left school, we still maintain a connection that was forged from the "glue" shared by many young men--immaturity, cockiness and uncertainty. Somehow, we found our way into manhood and have been able, by God's grace, to become responsible to the point that other people such as our wives, children, grandchildren and friends have been able to depend upon us. That is such a great feeling and makes us proud and humble at the same time. There is a line in a Larry Norman song that, when I hear it, I think of Bill and me. The song is "Song for a Small Circle of Friends" and the line is about his longtime friend Randy Stonehill. It says: "…and I still love him as we both crawl toward the lamp."

What I appreciate most about Bill is that, for me, he models Jesus Christ. I am more like Peter, the disciple. I'm the guy who wants to beat up the idiots around me; go to war and crush those who I feel are in need of a "tune-up." Bill and I have had discussions (primarily about our personal family matters) in which I say things like, "Bill, I just want to slap that guy." Bill, like Jesus, is calm and level-headed. He'll respond with 29 better ideas on how to handle it. His suggestions keep me out of jail and allow the potential target to retain his health.

When I first met Bill, I did not consider that we would still be friends after thirty-plus years because at nineteen, boys do not think about stuff like that. As we grew older and got married (not to each other!), we shared the bond of being apartment managers across the street from one another in San Jose. We were both flower delivery drivers for the same florist. Both of us worked in Juvenile Hall for the probation department where I have remained all these years. Bill and Janean moved away and our friendship lagged somewhat due to the distance. But one thing that I've always appreciated is that when we are again in the presence of one another, we pick up right where we left off, as if we have been in the same proximity the entire time. A love we share is photography and I am so impressed by Bill's skill in this. He has what photographers refer to as "the eye." I love looking at his pictures.

I may be able to "hold my own" with him in photography, but I cannot hold a candle to Bill as a theologian. He is very well read. Recently, on a houseboat trip to Lake Shasta, I overheard Bill and one of the other guys discuss the teaching of philosophers and theologians I have never even heard of. I am unable to participate in such talks due to the fact that I don't read Socrates or Perrin. When these discussions begin, I just say, "Let me know when you guys want to talk about cage fighting, redneck jokes or the joys of eating a Big Mac."

I am much honored to be called Bill's friend. I have benefitted from his generosity and his mutual love for me. He has shared with me some of his ministry experiences which I have put to use in my personal and professional life as a probation officer. The way he lives his life challenges me to be a better man and a more faithful Christian. His humility inspires me as we both crawl toward the lamp. I love you, Billy D. Thanks for calling me your best friend.

Rick Criscione grew up in San Jose and attended Yerba Buena High School from which he graduated in 1976, making him about one year younger than me. I count Rick as one of my best friends and closest confidants. We now live a couple of miles from each other and attend the same church.

I was already at SJBC when he arrived. I don't recall how we met, other than it was a small campus with about two hundred students in attendance. But we eventually got acquainted and became pals. Rick came to the school with two other guys he had grown up with--Mark Thompson and Rodney Williams--and there are stories about them, too, but that'll have to wait.

While we were in college, Rick and I decided to be roommates and began looking for an apartment. Another student, Steve Walker, said he was also looking for roommates and he had already put a deposit on a two-bedroom place one block from school at the "780's," which was an apartment complex inhabited by many other SJBC students. Rick and I would take one of the bedrooms and Steve took the other with an as-yet-to-be-named draft pick.

Prior to moving in, Steve interviewed some guys and settled on one guy from Los Alamos, New Mexico. Steve wanted Rick and me to meet him first so we four met in the apartment. My first impression of the guy was not the best based on his look and style of dress. He was short, wore glasses, and had thinning hair and a scraggly beard. He was very quiet and did not appear to be a good candidate. The fact he was wearing a navy blue pea coat gave me pause. In short, I was certain that this George Gardner guy was a drug user and maybe even a dealer. I later told Rick, "Man! That guy has been around the block! I don't know if I trust him to live with us." At this moment, I am laughing because I learned how far off base my first impression of him was. In spite of my objections, Steve wanted George to be his roomie and as the "owner" of the place, his wishes were respected. I have a couple of "George" stories which will also have to wait, but to make a long story short, not only had George NEVER used drugs, he had never been drunk or even tasted alcohol. He ended up, after college, also working for the Probation Department for more than twenty-five years. To this day, we are good friends.

One night Rick and I went to the Capitol Drive-In to see a movie. Rain was threatening but it waited until the movie was almost over before it began to sprinkle. It was late as we drove back to our apartment but we decided to stop off and see Rick's dad, Art, at his place of business. He worked at a bar called Mario's on Almaden Expressway where he was the head bouncer. I soon found why they wanted him for that job. It was a very rowdy place. Rick's dad was tough and his demeanor was intimidating. Obviously, he could handle the typical situations a bouncer encounters.

Rick and I went to the front door. Art was close to the door and when he saw us he told us to come on in so he could show us around. We walked through the club which was full of people who were drunk, laughing and having a good time. In one area he pointed to some small holes in the wall which had been put there by a patron the week before with his pistol. Apparently, the guy didn't want his wife dancing with the guy who got shot at. I asked Art if there were a lot of fights there. He acknowledged there were and that something bad happened almost every night.

After the short tour we headed for the exit so we could go outside to talk where it was quieter. As we were leaving, five guys came in who did not want to pay the cover charge. They were arguing with the woman who was taking the money. When one of them pushed her, it was on! Art grabbed the guy and told the other bouncers to get everyone outside. We all spilled through the exit out into the parking lot where a big fight between bouncers and would-be patrons erupted. I stood there not really knowing what to do. Rick's dad was knocking guys down and Rick was by his father trying to help him. By now, it was raining and the parking lot was wet and slippery.

At one point Art had a guy in a headlock and was jerking him around, all the while beating him about the head and face. Suddenly, one of the combatants pulled a pint of whiskey from his back pocket and cocked back his arm to throw it at Art. I was behind him a couple of feet so I reached out, grabbed the guy and pulled him back toward me. I socked him as hard as I could in the face and threw him to the pavement; the bottle broke in his hand as it hit the ground. The

190

guy was surprised and somewhat dazed so I thought the fight was over, but no. He stood up, retrieved a knife from his pocket and came toward me. I backed up and considered pushing him into the traffic that was speeding by on Almaden Expressway. Fortunately for me, a half dozen SJPD cars came screaming up and the guy took off at a run.

The officers arrested a couple of the guys and talked to Art who was well known to them due to his working at Mario's. A cop came over to Rick and me to get our story. He asked us our names and what our occupations were to which we answered we were college students. He asked, "What college?" Simultaneously, we hung our heads and mumbled, "San Jose Bible College." He didn't comment on that but I wondered what he thought about two Bible College students being at such a notorious bar, or any bar, for that matter. Rick's dad came over and told the officer that Rick was his son and we had come by to say hello. We were released at the scene.

A couple of years ago, I wrote this letter to Rick:

Dear Rick,

As I was getting ready for church this morning, you came to my mind. I began to think about what a faithful servant you are to the Ceres Christian Church congregation. You are there week in and week out heading up the team of deacons and ushers. You make sure that there is enough communion emblems to go around, you count the attendees and you assure that the building temperature is set at a comfortable level. Some people might not think these tasks are very significant, but I do. Your service in this area is important to the smooth operation of Sunday mornings. Thank you for your service.

One of the original dudes is Mark Thompson, who is from San Jose. I've mentioned him before, but now I want to expound on him and our relationship a bit more. After leaving SJBC, Mark went to college at Pacific Christian College, now Hope International University in Fullerton, California. I can only guess that Mark moved to PCC so he could be closer to his all-time favorite band, The Beach Boys. The guy has every album they recorded, I believe, as well as hundreds of MP3 files. Nonetheless, Mark earned a degree in Marriage and Family Counseling (as well as surfing and In-N-Out cuisine). He then moved to Tucson where he was a youth pastor for a while. Eventually, he moved back to San Jose where we both went to work as Group Counselors in Juvenile Hall. Mark loved the kids with whom we worked but he greatly disliked the politics and bureaucracy of the place. While working there he got permission to interview some of the youngsters and used those interviews in earning his Master's degree in Counseling. He then went back to being a youth pastor in the Santa Cruz area and a couple of churches in the Portland area of Oregon.

As young bucks in our college days, we had a professor who was a youth pastor at Central Christian Church in San Jose. His name is Don Hinkle and he inspired those of us who wanted to be youth workers. Don had great stories of his experiences and we loved his classes. There was only one problem: we, as young ignorant twenty-somethings, believed Don was too old to be an effective youth pastor. He was "old" because he was in his mid-thirties at the time and to us this was ancient. Guess what? Mark is now fifty-seven years old and still working full-time as a youth pastor. He remains highly effective. Mark admits he has slowed down tremendously and wishes he could be doing some other church ministry but he sn't yet found a new calling. However, his love for the kids is great and they love him. He teaches them important life lessons by having experiences together. Every year he takes a large group to Mexico for a week to minister to the poor, work with kids in an orphanage, and build a house for a family. These young men and women get their hands dirty serving the poor on these trips. How many of us can say we have done similar things?

Once a month, Mark's youth group goes to downtown Portland to minister to the homeless folks living under a bridge. They give these folks "care packages" which include bottled water, food, personal hygiene items and socks as well as other clothing. Mark has done these activities with hundreds of kids over the years. Putting what the Bible teaches into hands-on action has really benefited the youngsters. Many of them have stated these outreaches have changed their lives. Mark's compassion for people inspires me and causes me to want to follow his example. He was a great support to me after Daniel died. When I thanked him for it, he reminded me that I was a great help to him several years earlier when his older brother Warren fell suddenly ill and died soon after. Being a friend of Mark has made me a better person. Now, before I get too mushy and say something silly like, "He completes me" I will lighten the moment by saying that as much as I love him, his taste in music is mostly weird. I love you, dude.

I'm truly sorry that I cannot write more about my many friends but space does not allow it. However, there are four more that cannot be overlooked. One of them is Wayne Ford from Marina, California. He came to SJBC at age sixteen, resulting in being the youngest student up until that time. We became friends who have kept in touch for more than forty years. The Lord blessed me greatly with Wayne's friendship. He is loyal, loves God and was the caretaker for both his parents for years before their deaths, serving them like no one else could. Wayne often teaches a Bible class at his church in Carmel, California. He is almost always the first one to arrive to the men's weekly Bible study so he can set up chairs and make the coffee. He is truly God's servant.

I did not think that Mike Huskey, from Vista, CA, and I would become lifelong friends when he came to SJBC because I didn't like him much at first. He was opinionated and sarcastic. I believe the problem was that I also possess those traits, so we clashed, at least in my mind. Over the years I have come to see that Mike is one of the nicest and most generous men I know. We both admit we are on the same wavelength nowadays and care deeply for one another. I am a better person by being friends with Mike.

Diane Comstock, another SJBC alum, is a dear friend. She was formerly a DJ at a couple of radio stations in San Jose and currently runs her family's drapery manufacturing business. At the risk of sounding sexist, I must say Diane is the funniest woman I have ever known. In fact, few men I know are funnier and she is such a hoot to talk to and to interact with on Facebook. Her sense of humor often hits me like a train. Her wittiness is unparalleled and to top it off, she loves her family, friends and God with all her heart.

I have known Darren Briggs since college but only recently have we become close friends. Darren has a very successful art reproduction business in Sebastopol, CA. Recently, the Charles Schulz museum in Santa Rosa contracted him to enlarge hundreds of Mr. Schulz's cartoon panels that now hang in the museum. Darren is a dear friend who would do anything for you. He sings like an angel and has a music collection that rivals those of most radio stations. To top it off, he is a biblical scholar who is really into philosophy and theology; things of which I am an ignoramus. In spite of this, we are good pals.

Chapter Nine

On June 20, 2012, our twenty-eight-year-old son, Daniel Kevin Faddis died.

His death rocked me to the very depths of my soul. It was shocking and devastating. I now can understand more clearly how deeply my mother was hurt when my brother Kevin died thirty-one years ago in a car crash. However, my pain has a different level because Daniel shot himself. Some people believe that Daniel did not mean to kill himself, that it was accidental. As for me, I do not know anything more than he was very careful about guns and whether he meant to or not, he is still gone from us.

This event has changed me forever. I will always be sad that we will never again verbally spar with one another, watch a "macho man" movie together or go on a houseboat trip and compete to catch the most fish. I will not have a grandson named after me or hold a little girl that Daniel fathered. Although I hurt for myself, I hurt even more for my Linda. She carried our only son for nine months, nursed him and raised him while I was at work seemingly all the time. I believe there is a bond between mothers and their children that men do not have. I hurt for Daniel's sisters who deeply loved their big brother as well as for his nephews who idolized their Uncle Daniel. I especially grieve for his fiancée, Michelle, to whom he would have been married on July 21, 2012.

The following section is copied from blog posts made after Daniel's death. They have been briefly edited, but are included in order and in the format of the blog rather than being rewritten.

As I mentioned in the Acknowledgment section, this book grew out of my blog. This part is a real-time account of how I felt at the time I wrote each entry and how I dealt with our son's suicide.

I do not blame myself for Daniel's death. I was the best father I knew how to be. I was not absent and I provided the things a Dad is supposed to give his family--food, shelter and protection. My son and I had a good relationship for which I will always be grateful. I am not mad at God but I have railed at Him for allowing it to happen. Nonetheless, I have relied on my Heavenly Father to get me through all the other untimely deaths of my family members. Since this is the worst, I will need Him now more than ever.

I figure that I have two choices. I can give up on life and allow Daniel's death to wilt me. Or, I can use it to become a stronger and more compassionate man. I want as much good to come from his death as is possible. One of those things is writing this blog. Time will show what I decide to write here and if it will touch others. I am known to be a transparent person. I say what I think, I cry easily and I care about people. So, if you plan to follow my blog, be prepared to look at what is inside me because I intend to hold nothing back.

We do not understand why Daniel did this. He had a lot going for him with his upcoming marriage, pursuing his Bachelor's degree in Criminal Justice and his job, which he loved. It is our belief in Christ that gives us confidence that Daniel is in heaven and waiting for us to join him when we pass on.

Friday, July 20, 2012

A number of people have asked me if I have had trouble sleeping. The answer is no. Sleep is a refuge. It allows me to shut out the reality we are living. While I may toss and turn, and wake up more than usual during the night, my sleep is usually deep. However, it is the waking up that hurts. I have vivid dreams that seem so real, but when I awake, Daniel's being gone is what I always think of first. It's almost like learning about his death for the first time over and over again.

Michelle and Daniel were set to be married tomorrow at the Prince of Peace Lutheran Church in Fremont, CA. Today, we should all be converging on the East Bay to attend the rehearsal for the wedding followed by a dinner that I was to host as the groom's father. It was going to be at BJ's Restaurant and I had such a grand picture of the evening in my mind. We expected thirty or forty people to be there and I was really looking forward to it. It would have been my night to shine as the proud father who would pick up the tab for the festivities. The groom's dad has it so easy.

Saturday, July 21, 2012

The Walker and Faddis families and their friends should all be getting ready for a wedding this evening. Instead, Michelle is in Disneyland with several of her wedding party; Daniel's groomsmen are elsewhere; several members of my family are at a beach in Northern California; and I am sitting in front of this computer at home. This is not how it should be. This ought to be a day filled with joy, anticipation and activity. For me it is a somber day. Those of us who were supposed to be in Fremont this evening has been forced by an act we had no control over, to change our plans and spend the day elsewhere.

Michelle and her Mom, Debi, came to visit us last week. While here, Michelle told us it was her plan to spend this day in the Happiest Place on Earth. I encouraged her to do so and am proud that she is there now with her supportive friends. I chose to be alone instead of going with Linda, Holly, Bryan and Judah to Dillon Beach to visit our close friends who would have been at the wedding today. Each one of us is where we want to be right now which, in my opinion, is therapeutic. Some might say *that my being alone is not a good thing; that I should be around others right now, and not moping about. Being alone is how I best handle my sadness. I am not distracted by what is going on around me. I can cry, or pray or think about the good memories I have of my beloved son whom I miss terribly.*

Our "thing" was to quibble about stuff. We each enjoyed pushing each others' buttons. We liked presenting information the other one did not know, no matter how trivial. Each of us ALWAYS wanted to be right. We did not like the same movies, music or TV shows the other one did, mostly due to the generation gap. Yesterday, I was browsing Netflix and saw Glee in the line-up. This is a show that I have NO INTEREST in, and knowing my son as well as I do, knew he wouldn't like it either. Out of curiosity, I watched the pilot from 2009 and thought it was pretty entertaining so I watched a couple more episodes. It occurred to me that Daniel would have ridiculed me for watching even one minute of it. I could just hear him giving me a bad time about it. Well, earlier today, I was texting with Michelle and mentioned this fact to her. She laughed and revealed Glee was a show Daniel did watch and I busted up laughing. Now, I have to decide if I will watch more of it or not.

Monday, July 23, 2012

I began making burial plans for Daniel today. His cremains are sitting on the floor in a plastic box near my desk next to his Navy graduation photo. I glance at them once in a while and shake my head. That my vibrant, funny, complex, opinionated, sheepdog son has been reduced to a pile of ashes is almost beyond comprehension. Today has been very tearful and I suppose there will many such days ahead. Sometimes I just want to scream.

Daniel will be interred at the San Joaquin Valley National Cemetery in Santa Nella, forty miles from here. It is the nearest veterans' cemetery and our family agreed that Daniel would have wanted to be buried there. The date has yet to be determined but Linda told me today she wants us to do it as soon as possible. I agree with her because it would take us one more step toward closure (whatever that is).

Tuesday, July 24, 2012

After I retired last year I quickly found myself sitting around with nothing to do. I was bored and unmotivated to find stuff to occupy my time. I watched a lot of TV and surfed the web. Well, I thought that was bad, but this past couple of days have been even worse. I am lethargic and practically non-ambulatory. I realize this is not healthy but I don't really care. Some friends have tried to get me to go out and do something active but I always decline. I've missed the past five weeks of church because I don't want to face people right now. I'm not ready to take on the next wave of sympathy from those I have not seen face to face since Daniel died. I want to be a hermit right now.

I can hear Daniel saying, with that little smirk on his face that indicated he was half kidding me, "Hey, Old Man, why are you letting this get to you so much? Suck it up and move on." My answer to him would be something like, "Because it's how I want to be right now and I'll suck it up when I'm good and ready." My family has been good about leaving me alone when they see that's what I want. At other times, we talk about Daniel, recall fond memories of days gone by and support each other as we become sad and cry.

Linda and I have grown even closer together as we have gone through this but I don't recommend it as a method to strengthen a marriage. On the other hand, I am grateful to God who brings good from something so terrible.

Thursday, July 25, 2012

As I was looking through my computer today, I found this partially completed letter I wrote to Daniel just before he went into the Navy. He was nineteen years old then. How ironic that only nine years later I am saying goodbye to him again until that great day when we are reunited again. I do not recall if I gave this to him. Probably not, as it looks unfinished and is not signed. I post the letter here for your consideration:

July 23, 2003

My Dear, One and Only, Beloved Son,

This letter has been long in coming. I have begun it, in my mind, many, many times. It will take me a while to write it but I will finish before you leave. I already miss you and you have not even left yet.

Time has gone by so very quickly. It was just yesterday you were two years old and we were wrestling on the bed. You were such a little squirt! Now, you are grown up and have become a man. I treasure the moments I remember when you were small; when you looked at me in awe and truly believed I was the greatest man who ever lived.

One of my favorite memories is when I came home from salmon fishing and you were so excited I had caught a fish. I remember how proud and excited you were to hold up that fish as if you had been the one to catch it. I love thinking about how curious you were about everything.

Son, you have turned out to be a great and loving person. I never dreamed I would have a son like you. One who would be so handsome, smart and caring. I am so sad you are leaving, but am equally proud of what you have chosen to do for your country.

We had a good talk today about you, the Navy, being a cop, life, etc. I am glad you chose to be honest with me. I have always appreciated that about you. I think it makes our relationship stronger. It is hard for me to hear about the unwise choices you make; the ones you make in spite of my counseling and warnings. But, I also know you have to make your own decisions and learn some things the hard way. That is like real life I suppose, but some of those lessons will be very difficult to deal with so, again, I remind you to please listen to what I say and follow my advice.

Friday, July 27, 2012

After posting yesterday's blog entry I got to thinking about the relationship between father and son. Daniel and I had many talks about life and what we should do as we go through it. This involves being responsible; holding a job; providing protection, housing, food and the other necessities for loved ones; being law abiding; not hurting others, especially our wives and children; not taking advantage of anyone. We talked about how I had disappointed my Mom (my Dad died when I was eleven) and how Daniel had sometimes not lived up to my expectations and not followed my instruction. Sometimes he made me so angry with his behavior (which I will talk about more in the future) and even though I loved him, sometimes I did not like him. Then, today, I realized that no matter how much he angered me, or did not follow my counsel, or broke the "house rules" repeatedly, I still loved him. When he asked me to forgive him I did- -every time. I loved my son and I forgive him for his last, terrible mistake. A choice which cannot be reversed has caused so many of us searing pain, a choice for which he cannot ask forgiveness. Yet, I forgive him because I love him so much. He is my flesh and blood. He is my son.

God loves us in the same way and even more than we can possibly understand. If we could only comprehend that God loves us like we love our children, we would be better off. Many of us view God as sitting on his throne and looking down with condemnation, waiting for us to "mess up." If we do not do this to our own kids, why do we believe that God would treat us this way? He wants his to see him as "Abba" or "Daddy." This is how I choose to see him. Yes, He can be stern and angry. He allows us to make our own decisions knowing sometimes those choices hurt us. He is sometimes disappointed in how we live our lives. But, he is always there, waiting with open arms when we decide to run to Him and ask forgiveness. I am so glad to have a Heavenly Father like that and it inspires me to be an Earthly father like that to my children.

Sunday, July 29, 2012

Today I was thinking of another great connection Daniel and I shared. There were certain TV shows and movies that we liked to watch. If we couldn't watch them together, we talked about them later by telephone. Some of our favorites were Southland, Boardwalk Empire, Homeland *and* Band of Brothers. *There were others that he liked and I didn't such as* House *and* South Park. *I liked* Lost *and* Friday Night Lights *but he didn't. There were certain movies that we agreed to only see together the first time and often we went to the first showing available on opening day. These included* Saving Private Ryan, Shooter, Four Brothers *and* Gladiator. *The last movie we saw together was* Warrior. *We were both Mark Wahlberg fans.*

We enjoyed discussing the movie or TV episode and the great characters that the writers had created. We both liked the character John Cooper (played by Michael Cudlitz) in Southland *a lot. He also portrayed Sgt. Denver "Bull" Randleman in* Band of Brothers. *This is a simple connection we had but I will always treasure it. It gives me something to hold on to about him and me.*

I will also hold on to one trip we took when Daniel was about thirteen. My brother Jeff, Daniel and I went to Sitka, Alaska to fish on my friend's salmon boat. We flew from San Jose to Juneau and took the ferry to Sitka. We caught fish until we were too tired to reel them in. We flew back to San Jose a week later. Each of us brought back a seventy-pound box of salmon and halibut fillets that were vacuum packed and flash frozen. It was the greatest trip the three of us ever took together.

I cannot think of the Alaska trip without remembering that in 2000 our family of six (Linda, Daniel, Heather, Holly, Meagan and I) went to Maui for eleven days. On about the fifth day there, we went to Big Beach where Daniel, Heather and I boogie boarded. I got slammed into the beach by a huge wave and fractured six ribs and punctured my lung. This earned me a thirteen day stay in the hospital on Maui. I remember sitting on the beach in excruciating pain, waiting for the rescue workers to arrive. My sixteen-year-old son, with tears streaming down his face, looked into my eyes and said, "Dad, I love you so much and I don't want to lose you!" What a beautiful thing to hear from a child. It's a memory I will always cherish.

Sunday, August 12, 2012

One of the first thoughts that drifted into my mind when I woke up this morning is that right now I do not care if I live or die. There is no way I would take my own life, especially after having had to live through this past seven weeks. Suicide wrecks so many people around the deceased. However, if I dropped dead from a heart attack or a car crash I am ready for it. Being in heaven would be so much better than this staying in this world. Heaven means no pain, no sadness, and no worries. The depression and sadness are so debilitating. I have no ambition and no desire to get some. There is nothing more that I feel like accomplishing each day other than to get out of bed and most days that is not until 10 or 11.

Later in the morning, I called Linda into where I was sitting because I was on the verge of losing it and I needed her to console me. She stood there in front of me and cradled my head for a long time as I cried and told her how I feel. I said through my tears and pain, "God! Please take me or fix me! I cannot take this hurt!" Linda, crying also, said, "You can't fix a broken heart." She is so right. Before this happened to us, I believed that something like this would have just taken time to get over and that the hurt would subside. Now, I no longer believe such. I don't know when, if ever, the pain will go away. Right now, the best I can hope for is that I will learn to manage the pain and figure out how to keep it from managing me.

Just now, as I was typing this, my five-year-old grandson, Logan, who is visiting us this week, came to me and whispered, "Grandpa, don't tell anyone in this house, but I think you are the best grandpa in the world." Sometimes, I guess, God sends five-year-old angels to take our eyes off ourselves so we can see the bigger picture.

Thursday, August 16, 2012

Today is Thursday and this morning I realized that the last couple of days have been better for me. I have not thought about Daniel and his suicide as much. I have shed fewer tears. I cannot say that I am "over it" but I am hopeful that I am making progress. As I stated in my last post, I want to learn to manage my pain rather than allow my pain to manage me.

Today, Linda and I had lunch with our pastor Adam Miller and his wife, Jenn. Adam asked Linda how she was doing to which she answered, "I am staying busy." I need to take a lesson from her and get busy. If I do so, I will have less time to dwell on the circumstances.

I am very grateful for the many expressions of support, love and prayer we have received from people. We have been told that folks all over the world, most of whom do not even know us, are praying for us. We, in turn, are praying for the suffering and tragedy of people we do not know. The prayer network that can be created is immense. And it is expanded exponentially by way of the internet. This network has helped us so much because I know that God hears the prayers of hundreds on our behalf. It causes me to be conscious of my own need to pray for others. If I take the time to pray for my fellow humans, I am doing something productive, I am busy, and it takes my mind off me for a while. I encourage you to pray for others because it will benefit them and you too.

Wednesday, August 22, 2012

Yesterday I was talking with a good friend, Chris Blair, who is a pastor in Oregon. He and his wife, Debbie came to visit us while they're on vacation to support us as we continue to grieve. We discussed the importance of telling others what we appreciate about them. The people we meet in life (friends, casual acquaintances, co-workers, family, even strangers) truly appreciate it when we compliment them. This is very important for us to do since we live in such a negative and critical environment.

Since Daniel died, I have had so much love from people who tell me what a great guy I am and how much my kindness has helped them. This has helped me tremendously and I want to uplift others even more than I have in the past. I hope that my mentioning it here will encourage you to do the same. Don't wait for something terrible to happen to someone you know until you "love on them." Smile at strangers, say hello to everyone you meet, tell your Mom and Dad, your friends, your siblings, your "better half" something you appreciate about them. They will be edified.

Sunday, August 26, 2012

Shortly after Daniel died, my friend Bill Dobos, gave me a book titled Lament for a Son, *written by Nicholas Wolterstorff. The book is about the author's grief after losing his son in a mountain climbing accident. There is so much in this book to which I can relate. The boy's death was unexpected; he was twenty-five, Daniel was twenty-eight; his father sometimes got angry with him over the boy's self-centeredness, etc.*

In one chapter, Wolterstorff speaks about his friend whose son committed suicide a few weeks before his own son died. Following is from his book and is worth repeating here:

The pain of his [the friend's son's] life was so intense that he took the life that gave the pain. I thought for a time that such a death must be easier to bear than the one with zest for life. He wanted to die. When I talked to the father, I saw that I was wrong.

Death is the great leveler, so our writers have always told us. Of course they are right. But they have neglected to mention the uniqueness of each death – and the solitude of suffering which accompanies that uniqueness. We say, "I know how you are feeling." But we don't.

Wednesday, August 29, 2012

Earlier today I was sitting in the living room watching TV. My seven-month-old grandson, Judah, was lying on the floor on a blanket. He is learning to turn over and get up on his hands and knees. He can crawl somewhat but not in a forward direction. He's good at going sideways and backwards, though.

As I contemplated how quickly he is growing and developing, something occurred to me I had never considered before. Being a grandpa is way more fun than being just a dad. As a grandfather who is retired I have much time to interact with and observe my four grandchildren. Since Judah and his parents live with us, I have a lot of time to be with him and I love it. As a young father to our own children I had far less time with my kids due to working all the time to support them. Leaving for work in the morning and coming home at night, shortly before their bedtime, did not leave much room for being with them.

Daniel was six months old when I went to work part-time for the Santa Clara County Probation Department. I was eager to make a living for my small family and I hustled to get as many hours as possible. In June 1985 I was hired full-time and worked forty hours per week plus all the overtime I could grab because our daughter Heather was set to arrive in August of that year. Holly came on the scene in May 1987. Linda was able to stay home with our children because I made good money and worked a lot. She had the good fortune to see all the things about our kids' growing up that I missed.

However, I am now able to see what I missed and I am so appreciative of this. I used to joke that being a grandparent was good because when the kid cried or pooped, you could hand him or her back to their mom or dad. Today, I realized how truly wonderful it is to be a grandpa. I also learned again how important it is to spend time with our kids and grandchildren because we don't know how long we will have together.

Saturday, September 1, 2012

Several days ago, our daughter Holly posted the below paragraph regarding Daniel on her Facebook page:

Facebook leaves this section blank and asks "What's on your mind?" To which I answer: My brother. My amazing, kind, funny, loving, protecting, big brother. I wish you were here to comfort and hug me as you have done before. But then again, if you were here, I wouldn't be crying.

Her post was commented on by the following people:

Eric Hill (Daniel's and Holly's friend):

But Holly he is still doing it. Just because we can't see it, it's a feeling and when we least expect it, that feeling overcomes us. What that feeling is, is him holding you from Heaven.

Deania Celli (Daniel's classmate at UOP):

Your brother was bigger than life and even though he is gone physically, he will never truly be gone. I never realized how much your brother touched my life. I don't think I could have made it through class without him. I am glad to call him my friend. I miss his jokes, some so bad you just had to laugh. I wish I had the chance to tell him I am glad he was my friend.

Michael Pritchard (Life coach, comedian and my friend for thirty years):

Your brother was and still is an angel force standing guard in his Master at Arms uniform; strong, kind, loving protector of goodness. He has and never will leave you or your family! Think of him in heaven where he stands guard over goodness, truth and the love of

God in Christ! PRITCHARDS ARE PRAYING FOR YOU ALL.

Shawn Strannigan (Family friend who lost her four-year old son in a car accident):
> Keep talking, crying, remembering, Holly! We always ache a little more for Jonah on this day (anniversary of the car crash). A reminder to cover you all in prayer today . . .

Brittani Loveall (Holly's cousin):
> So sorry, Holly. I'll say a prayer for you today. I can't even begin to understand what you all are going through. May God wrap you in His arms and give you comfort and peace. Love you Holly. P.S. my mom and I are talking about making a trip up there next week...

Heather Masamitsu (Holly's and Daniel's sister):
> That was me last night Hobbs. I miss him so much. I think it hurts more now than it did at first. I just keep telling myself it won't be this bad forever and hold onto that.

Michelle Walker (Daniel's fiancée):
> It has been really hard for me this week, too. I miss him so much everyday it is even more then the day before. It has been getting worse but it will get better with time. It is just going to take a very, very long time. I love you and have been praying for you! Call me if you need anything.

Reading these posts helped me to again see how much others are also hurting. It seems to come in waves, ebbing and flowing. No day is the same as the day before. But, I also noticed the hope that we will not always ache so badly. Another thing I see here is the incredible support we give to one another. I thank God for His love and mercy which He shows us through our family and friends.

Wednesday, September 5, 2012

This afternoon, Linda and I drove to the San Joaquin Memorial Cemetery in Santa Nella to see where we will bury Daniel's cremains next week. The sprawling cemetery is for veterans and their spouses. Neither of us has ever been there before and Linda was surprised to see that there are no standing markers. She expected to see hundreds of white crosses marking the graves as depicted in the movie Saving Private Ryan. *The markers at SJV are all flat rectangles made of a cement-type material. The nearby brown hills along I-5 are a stark contrast to the beautiful, thick green sod of the burial grounds. It is remote and peaceful. Daniel will be happy we are putting him in a place surrounded by other vets with similar ideals to his own. I counted approximately a dozen groundskeepers maintaining the area and preparing to lay fresh sod around the new graves. Judging by the size of the place and the number of workers, this is a busy place.*

Daniel's memorial service back in June was a beautiful and special time of remembrance attended by some four hundred people. Here, it will be very short. Linda will read a heartbreaking, yet healing piece she wrote titled, "Whispering Hope." I will say a couple of words and lead a prayer. The "service" will be attended by only the family, his fiancée, her family and several of their closest friends. Due to the cemetery's strict rules, there are no graveside services. We will be assigned a "shelter" where we will conduct our final ritual. His cremains will have already been given to the personnel along with the proper paperwork as well as what we want to have included on his marker. He will be buried sometime later that day and his marker will be placed thirty to sixty days later. The marker will include his name, birth/death dates, his military service and the following inscription: "Beloved son, brother, uncle, fiancé and friend."

As we went on our "mission" today, we both felt a renewed sense of loss. Linda commented that next Friday will be very difficult for her. We both agreed that we will feel relief that the next "chapter" in this sad, sad event will come to a close.

I have buried many of my family including my parents, grandparents, and three siblings. However, today's task was so surreal for me. As we drove through the cemetery entrance it hit me like a ton of bricks that this is the place my only son will rest and how unfair it is that I, his father, have to bury him and not the reverse. I do not understand the ways of the world, why things happen and other such mysteries. But, I rest assured knowing that God, the creator of the universe, the giver and taker of life is in full control and that someday I will understand. Rest in peace my beloved son.

Tuesday, September 11, 2012

I vividly recall where I was on this day eleven years ago when I learned of the attack on our nation. I walked into work that morning and saw several co-workers watching a TV that showed the first plane hit the tower. Our first thought was that it was an accident, but then the second one hit the other tower and a sick feeling hit us that the actions were intentional. It was unbelievable then that this had happened. It still boggles the mind eleven years later.

9/11 also marks a different anniversary for me because it was nine years ago today that my then-nineteen-year-old son reported for duty to the U.S. Navy. This was not by happenstance that he reported on this anniversary of the attack. He and his buddy, Travis Grover planned it that way. I cannot speak for Travis but I knew that Daniel worked it out because it was so important to him. It is also my belief that the 9/11 attack was a big factor in Daniel wanting to join the military.

I recall how proud I was of him for enlisting. Yes, I was concerned about his safety but this was outweighed by everything else. Daniel, like his father, struggled with a weight problem. The Navy recruiter saw to it that Daniel was ready the day he reported. He met with Daniel and Travis (who did not need the extra attention) frequently to run and condition. He was ready physically and mentally to join up.

I cried like a baby when he left for Great Lakes, Illinois and waited impatiently to hear from him. Upon his arrival there he was given a thirty-second telephone call home to say he was there. I wanted to hear all about his trip and how everything was going but it was not allowed. He said he had to go and the call was cut off. It was days before we had further contact and not a minute went by that I did not think of him.

According to the Naval Historical Center at the Washington Navy Yard, there is no official motto for the U.S. Navy. Non Sibi Sed Patriae ("Not Self But Country"), Paratus et Potens ("Ready and Able"), & Semper Fortis ("Always Courageous") are often cited as the Navy's motto.

The term Non Sibi Sed Patriae ("Not self but country") is inscribed over the entrance to the Chapel at the U.S. Naval Academy in Annapolis, Maryland. It's likely that's where the belief that it's the Navy's motto originates.

Daniel spent three years in the Navy. Twenty-two months of that time he was in the Persian Gulf as part of Operation Iraqi Freedom. It was something he really desired to do and it took a lot of work for him to get into shape. Words cannot express how proud I am of my boy for making this commitment.

Monday, September 17, 2012

Last Friday, Linda and I buried our son. Even though we had already had a memorial service in June, the actual burial was the harder of the two. However, some innocent comedic relief was provided by our five-year-old grandson Logan that I want to share. As I sat on my bed getting dressed, Logan came in to talk to me. He and his brother Luca had already been advised about Daniel's passing as well as that he had "accidentally" shot himself. Logan knew we were going to a ceremony and to bury Uncle Daniel. He asked, "Grandpa, where is Daniel?" I admitted that he was in our house. His eyes got wide and he said, "Where are you hiding him?" I tried my best not to laugh and said I would show him after I got dressed. He begged me to confide in him and promised not to tell anyone. He said we can do a "pinky swear," so we did and I said Daniel was in my office. A bit later, Luca came in and said Logan had told him. So much for pinky swears.

Later, I showed them the urn and Logan, ever the thinker, said, "How did you squish him in there?" I said I would tell him later, when he was older. The two boys rode with Linda and me to the cemetery. Halfway there, out of the blue, Logan started tearing up and said, "I wish I was there when Uncle Daniel shot himself because I could have told him to point the gun the other way!" You and me both, little man.

When we all arrived at the San Joaquin Memorial Cemetery, we parked in a staging area and drove in a processional to the committal shelter to have our service. I read two scriptures and led a prayer. Linda read something she wrote which is so eloquent, sad and hopeful. She titled it "Whispering Hope" and it appears below:

It is a matter of irreconcilable understanding as to whether this act of Daniel's was intentional or not. Either way, it is done and he is gone and we are left to live without him. These past few months have given me much to think about. As a mother, I would like to share the following with you with the intent that you would find both encouragement and that you would look very hard at your own life.

First of all, many people and religions believe that suicide means you can't go to heaven. They call it the "unforgivable sin." I do not believe this and I think I can prove this with Scripture. God is merciful and gracious. He is also just. We will be judged, not on the nature of our death, but rather on the nature of our lives.

I can't answer why. Stan had spoken with Daniel several times that day. Jason had just talked to him shortly before it happened. Michelle was there when it did happen. NO ONE can answer why it occurred. Please don't try. It is futile. The question we MUST answer is how are we going to live our lives from here on out. Some of us are parents of adult children, some are grandparents, some are parents of young children, some are getting married, and some may never get married. We may face death, disease, heart ache, and great disappointment at any time. Life happens. I know without a doubt that this event would have been so much harder if I didn't have God's Spirit with me daily.

In July, I drove to San Jose and as I was coming into Milpitas I got stuck in traffic resulting from an accident. In short, a car towing a boat trailer carrying a boat was heading north. The trailer broke free and hit the center divider sending the boat flying across the divider into southbound traffic, striking another vehicle. The boat was decimated. The vehicle was totaled. I don't know what happened to the driver of the vehicle or if there were any passengers. It didn't look good though. My point is, metaphorically speaking, we never know when the boat is going to fly through the air and hit us--maybe taking our life.

Everyone here knows God and Jesus to some extent. Daniel did too. Was he living his life in a way that honors God? You can answer that in various ways. It's his turn now to stand in judgment before God and give an answer for his life. Someday, it will be our turn. I don't want to give statements of hope as to how he entered eternity. That's between him and God. I do know without a doubt though he now knows God fully and has fallen on his face in remorse for his life and in absolute love and thankfulness for what Jesus did for him on the Cross.

I am pleading with everyone here to learn from Daniel's life. He was a son, grandson, brother, nephew, friend, lover, almost son-in-law, brother-in-law, and uncle. He made us laugh. He made us frustrated and angry. He gave and he took. Please examine thoroughly your actions, words, and how they affect those around you; and especially examine your relationship with Jesus and be all you can be in Christ--because without Him we can do nothing.

After the service, we drove over to the area where he was to be buried and stood by our cars to watch as a caretaker laid our son to rest. He then motioned us over to gather around the grave. It was a beautiful and touching time.

Sunday, October 28, 2012

Linda and I went to the cemetery today to visit Daniel's grave. I sat in the truck as I am unable to walk up the small hill on the thick grass without fear of falling down. Daniel is buried about one hundred feet from the road. Linda went and stood there for a while. This was a good thing because I believe she needed some time alone with our son. She came back to the truck and we held each other while we cried.

Although the pain of our loss has begun to subside, we have moments when it hits us again that our son is gone from this world; out of reach. Gone is his presence, his largeness of life, his dry sense of humor and his gentleness which he attempted to hide under a rough exterior.

These moments of sadness hit us without expectation. When they come to me, I cry for a bit and then get myself under control. Last week, I opened a drawer and there was a picture of him on top that I had put in there and forgotten. Certain songs get me. One of these is a Don Williams song titled, "If Hollywood Don't Need You, I Still Do." Back when he was in high school, he had a girlfriend whom he missed terribly while our family was on a houseboat trip. I let him listen to the song, which he had never heard before, on my iPod. It's a real tearjerker if you're hurting like he was. He must have listened to that song five-hundred times on that trip while he moped around for the week. Now, whenever I hear it, it tears me up, but it also makes me smile because it tells me I helped my boy get through a difficult time.

When our kids were small, one of their favorite things to watch on the VCR was a cheesy recording of Peter Pan. It is a stage play starring Mary Martin as Peter. A song from that movie is "Tender Shepard" that the kids and mom sing together as a lullaby. After Daniel died I was going through his iPhone looking at his music. This song was in there which made our family laugh and then cry. To me, it shows Daniel's tender nature. Of course, this song will now be very special to me.

As I have said before, I look forward to the day when I enter heaven (hopefully, many years from now) and find my son waiting for me. This is what keeps me going, wanting to have good relationships with all *my family and friends so that we can all look forward to seeing one another on the other side. As I am writing this, I am reminded of something Daniel often said, "See you later; if not, I'll see you on the other side." Roger that MA3 Daniel Faddis.*

Tuesday, October 30, 2012

The majority of my ramblings on this blog have revolved around Daniel's death and life. This is natural, I suppose, as he is why I started the blog. Most of the writings have dealt with my grief, crying, and general sadness. There has been a taste of fond thoughts, hope at seeing him in heaven and humor, but it has mostly been negative things. As I have said, I don't know how long I will grieve to this extent, but these moments are winding down in number and intensity. For this, I am grateful.

Yesterday, I began to give some thought to the bright side of my life which led me to the other members of my immediate family. From the youngest, Caedence, my sweet and newest baby girl who is only a month old; Judah, my nine-month-old grandson who is crawling everywhere and pulling himself up to a standing position; Cambria (nineteen months) who does the "pretty girl" dance, runs to give me hugs and loves to play chase; Logan the five-year-old future UFC fighter who is hooked on all things Godzilla and who jumps up to sit next to me without prompting; Luca my seven-year-old deep thinker, future doctor or lawyer who is the most awesome Lego builder I have ever had the pleasure of knowing.

These five grandchildren were birthed by my two extraordinary daughters, Heather and Holly. Judah is Holly's son; the two girls and the other two boys are Heather's. Currently, Holly and Judah live with us so I get to see them interact almost daily. Holly is a great Mom who talks sweetly to Judah, calling him "Bug." She makes him laugh a lot and it is a joy for me to watch them together. Sometimes they play chase with Grandma Linda who holds Judah as she "runs" away from Holly. Good times.

Heather's mom skills are awesome and she needs every bit of them to deal with her four kids. I call Luca and Logan "Comanches" due to their wildness. Cambria adores them and wants to do everything her big brothers do. Caedence is nursing and she can scream louder than any infant I have ever heard. Heather takes all this in stride and handles all four very well. She is also a doula (look it up) and is training to be a midwife.

My daughters are awesome; they have big hearts, care about others and love their Daddy. I am so proud of how they are raising their children. I am prouder to be their father. They are not great mothers by happenstance. They learned from the best. Linda is a great mom and an even better grandma. She loves her babies with a passion and it shows by how she interacts with the four who live in Sebastopol when they are visiting us. She takes Luca, Logan, Cambria and Judah on walks to the park, plays games with them and invents all sorts of fun things for them to do.

Yes, I have many "bright spots" in my life and I am so grateful to God the Father who has blessed me so richly. I encourage anyone who is facing adversity to look for the bright things in your life.

Personal note to my sons-in-law Sam Masamitsu and Bryan Nani: I didn't mention you above because, uh . . . I couldn't think of anything to say. (= Treasure your blessings, boys.

Thursday, November 8, 2012

Thanksgiving 2012 will be here soon and it will be a bittersweet time for our family. Some of us have commented about not having Daniel here at the table. This, I think, was his favorite holiday. It was in the top two, I am sure. It is special to all of us because we have been so blessed to have had many Thanksgiving holidays together. I will do my best this year not to be in a somber mood, primarily for the sake of my family. They are affected by how I feel and if I am "up" they are likely to also be that way. As the leader, I want us all to have a good time. I want us to remember that Daniel is at peace and in a much better place. There are new memories for us who remain to build. My daughters have their own spouses and children now to begin their own catalogs of thoughts, fond memories and thankfulness. So, even though we will be hurting, we can have a great Thanksgiving Day this year.

I am thankful for so much and I try to tell God this sometimes when I think about it. First, He has promised me eternal life with Him because I have accepted his Son, Jesus as my Savior. This is the greatest gift of all. Then, here on Earth he has given me (at least) fifty-five years of life, a beautiful wife of thirty-two years, wonderful children, beautiful grandchildren who love me so much and many friends and extended family. I have traveled to Tahiti, Hong Kong, China, the Caribbean and Hawaii as well as many parts of the United States. I have done a lot of fun stuff such as being a professional sports photographer, a bodyguard to Robin Williams for a day, a Christian concert photographer who has been published in a magazine, and I got to be in college for eight years (=.

For the past two weeks I have been thankful for not living in the path of Hurricane Sandy and suffering the way so many of those poor people are. My heart aches for them. I hope they will get the help they need from the government and others to help them rebuild. However, I know that most will never regain what they have lost. The devastation is too huge. I do not talk much about my political views in public. I have little trust in politicians of both parties because I believe so many of them are corrupted by the "power" they have been granted. The problems are far and away too big to be fixed by humans. I see the United States as going down the same path as other powerful societies in history such as the Greeks and the Romans. However, even though I think harsh and scary times are coming to our country, I will continue to trust in God who is my Savior. He is the King of kings and the Lord of lords. I need Him to lean on right now while going through this time of my son's suicide; I will need Him for the unseen problems and heartaches that lie ahead. Some of the possibilities include terrorist attacks, devastating earthquakes, losing my pension or the *untimely death of other family members. I don't dwell on these things, but I know they are all possible.*

In the Bible, 2 Chronicles 7:14 says, "If my people, who are called by my name, shall humble themselves, and pray, and seek my face, and turn from their wicked ways; then will I hear from heaven, and will forgive their sin, and will heal their land." I believe this scripture with all my heart. I wish all of us believed it and followed its instruction because if we did, our country would be a much better place. Lord, please heal our land.

Thursday, December 13, 2012

My daughter, Heather called me today with a sad story. My seven-year-old grandson, Luca was drawing a picture last night and as he did so he was crying. Heather heard him and went over to see what was going on. It depicted Luca and his Uncle Daniel standing side by side, each with a broken heart over their heads. Another panel showed a grave with Luca standing at its foot. Heather asked Luca about his picture. He replied that he really misses his Uncle Daniel and wishes he was still here. Hearing this broke my heart. This is not the first time Luca or his little brother Logan has, out of the blue, mentioned Daniel and his death. Each time they do, it again brings the pain of this event to the surface. While I am sad for myself, my heart aches for these little guys who loved him so much.

Folks, if you ever consider taking your own life, please think again and again and again. Consider how detrimental your death will be to your family and friends. Ponder the mess you will leave behind regarding your possessions, obligations and everything else. But think most of all, about how important you are to someone else. For some, like Daniel, this will be many as evidenced by the hundreds that came to his memorial service. Or, it may be only a few, but we ALL have someone in our life who loves us whether it is a spouse, sibling, parent or friend.

Eventually, Luca will move on and his memory of Uncle Daniel will fade as will the pain he is experiencing right now. But for now he is hurting and that is such a sad thing. And it could have been avoided had Daniel taken into consideration the future ramifications of his rash act.

Sunday, March 10, 2013

Playing "Christian"

A game that kids like to play is "House." This is the game where young children pretend that they are grownups, set up a pretend household and assume the roles of the father, mother, the children, uncles and aunts, etc. Sometimes the kids like to pretend they are the family dog or cat.

Allow me to take a rabbit trail here and relate a story my daughter Heather told me about my grandson Logan who is six years old... As she drove him to school Friday morning, Logan said, "Mom, I have a lot of friends that are girls." Heather then said, "Yup. That's okay; just remember to treat them like ladies." He replied, "Right. I should treat them like they are my wife." When Heather asked him how he would do that, he said, "Treat them kindly and make sure they have enough food to eat." That's my boy!

Today, I will admit to you all that, for most of my life, much like children playing "house," I have played "Christian." I have not done my best all the time to follow the teachings of God's Word, the Bible. Primarily this is because of my penchant for chasing my own desires, my tendency for self-indulgence, and my willingness to be distracted by so many other things of the world. An example of this is the many hours I spend watching TV, playing video games, surfing the internet or reading fictional novels. Now, there really is nothing inherently wrong about these pastimes; however, I have allowed these things to take the place of doing more important tasks such as serving others, sharing the Gospel with those I come into contact with and, most importantly, reading God's Word. The Bible is how we get to know God. It's how He speaks to us.

I think that most of my friends and family who are followers of Christ would say, "Stan, you are doing a good job of following God. You are kind; you care about people and help them when you can." But I want more. I want to know God better. I want Him to be proud of me like a father wants to be proud of his son or daughter. I want to help more people come to Jesus so that they can spread the Gospel and ultimately go to heaven after our life on this planet is done. The Bible likens heaven to a wedding feast, which of course is a party. I sometimes say that I want to bring as many people as I can to that party.

Unfortunately, I get sidetracked by the reasons listed above. Even in my younger days, I knew I was putting off the most important tasks, but I just waved it away thinking I have so much more time ahead me and I'll do it later. Well, it is "later" right now, this minute, this week, this month. To define the tasks I speak of I have to share with you what the Bible calls "The Great Commission," which Jesus Christ gave to his disciples.

After Jesus Christ's death on the cross, he was buried and resurrected on the third day. Before he ascended into heaven, he appeared to his disciples in Galilee and gave them these instructions found in Matthew 28:18-20:

> Then Jesus came to them and said, "All authority in heaven and on earth has been given to me. Therefore go and make disciples of all nations, baptizing them in the name of the Father and of the Son and of the Holy Spirit, and teaching them to obey everything I have commanded you. And surely I am with you always, to the very end of the age." (NIV)

As the last recorded personal directive of the Savior to his disciples, it holds great significance to all followers of Christ. It is the foundation for evangelism and cross-cultural missions work in Christian theology. Because the Lord's instructions were to go to all nations and that he would be with us until the very end of the age, Christians of all generations have embraced this command. As many have said, it's not "The Great Suggestion." No, the Lord has commanded us to put our faith in action.

I think you'd agree with me that this is a pretty important directive and I've been ignoring it most of my life. Not completely, but mostly. And it is no longer acceptable. Although I might think of myself as a "mature" Christian, I have so much further to go. I have had numerous talks with my father-in-law, Reed Shackelford, who at age eighty-five still wrestles with "not doing enough." So, obviously, this is not just a young person's struggle. I recently told some Christian brothers in our men's Bible study that I am almost fifty-six years old and I regret not "doing more" all these years. I do not want to make it to age eighty-five and still be saying this. It's not right and it's not fair to God in light of what He has done for me. By continuing to allow self-indulgence to prevent me from following the Great Commission, I am missing out on so much! I want to again be excited about my faith. I desire to hunger for God. I want to crave reading my Bible, to share my faith with others and then work to make disciples.

Recently, I downloaded a book by Francis Chan to my Kindle, entitled Multiply. *It's a guide on how to make disciples and how to be a better one, too. I recommend it to those who are serious about following the Great Commission. It is my intention to put the teachings of this book to work with some of my friends at church. Hopefully, these men will, in turn, put what we will learn together to work in the lives of others who also hunger to serve God more fully.*

I am hoping that someone who reads this will be inspired to take this step with me. I need to be held accountable and encouraged to keep going. Even if you don't choose to make disciples yourself, please email me on occasion to check on my progress and tell me how you are doing in your walk with God. I can be reached at stanfaddis@gmail.com. Let's all stop playing "Christian." Thanks for your help.

Wednesday, March 27, 2013

Cadbury Eggs

Last night, Linda told me, "I want to go see Daniel tomorrow." It surprised me because her announcement was sudden and unexpected. I asked why, to which she replied, "Every Easter when the kids were little, I'd buy them some of those nasty Cadbury candy eggs. Daniel just loved them. I want to take him some for Easter."

So, this morning she got up and drove the forty miles to the San Joaquin Valley National Cemetery. She wanted to go alone and I did not object. Before leaving town, she stopped and bought the eggs. She sent me a photo of his gravesite with the eggs and it made me cry. The cap he wore while he served our country in the Persian Gulf is included in the photo, but she brought it home with her. She called me to say she was leaving the cemetery to head home and I could hear that she was crying. She later thanked me for letting her go alone and said she needed it. She said she has not cried that hard in several months.

I relate very well with her need to be alone with her son and her grief. Sometimes, we want to have others around us when we cry about our losses, but sometimes it is better to grieve in solitude. Until Linda told me of the Easter Cadbury egg tradition last night, I had no conscious recollection of it. I vaguely remember her giving the kids candy on Easter, but until now, did not know it was such a special memory for her. However, next year I will remember and that is a good thing; sad, but good.

Thursday, June 12, 2014

Two Years Gone

June 20, 2014, will mark the second anniversary of our son Daniel's suicide. Thinking about the 730 days that will have passed by that date causes me to wonder about the many things that could have occurred during that time span. These include the big events such as his marriage to Michelle, graduation from college, and maybe even Daniel becoming a father. It also includes the small, everyday stuff such as the celebration of birthdays, pool parties, BBQ's, fishing trips, going to the movies and the joking and laughter that is very commonplace around here.

As the time passes, I find myself being more appreciative of my relationships with my three daughters Heather, Holly and Meagan as well as my sons-in-law, Brian and Sam. The other day, Sam, Heather, their five children, dog and cat moved in with us. They are transitioning from the North Bay to the Central Valley to be closer to us, as well as Sam's parents and siblings who live in Southern California. They plan to live with us for a few months until they find just the right house for them here in Turlock. Linda and I are excited about it and all the chaos that is attached. It's great to have all of our kids so close by.

I've previously written about the hole in my life that Daniel's death created. It is deep and wide and void of all the wonderful things that it would have contained had he not died. However, as the time passes, I don't think of him as often as I did before and those moments of remembering him are not always as emotion-filled as they were in the past. This is not to say that there are no longer times when I break down and cry, but these moments have diminished in number and intensity.

As I ponder the above I realize that I need to stop dwelling on my loss and focus on all the great things that make up my life, of which there are many. These include Linda, my wife of nearly thirty-four years; three daughters; two sons-in-law; and, most of all, our seven grandchildren-- Luca, Logan, Cambria, Judah, Caedence, Joshua and Quinn. My blessings also include other family members, many close friends, a wonderful church family at Ceres Christian Church, a comfortable home and many other material possessions. I have had an incredible life so far and I hope that God will bless me with many more years here on this planet. After that, it only gets better for me: eternal life in the presence of the Creator, a perfect body that will never hurt or be sick again, reunification with loved ones that have gone before me, and new friends I will meet in heaven.

So, on June 20, 2014, I will wake up and think of Daniel and it will sadden me that he is gone, but then I will look at all the good things that God has blessed me with and I will smile and give Him the praise that only He deserves to receive.

Conclusion

A love letter to Linda:

*It has been so long since I wrote a love letter to you.
Sure, I have told you that I love you. I've written short notes and
quick words in Mother's Day and birthday cards. But I cannot
recall when the last time was that I wrote you a genuine love letter.
So, I'm writing it now.*

*You have heard me countless times tell the story of the
first time I saw you. I love to tell it because by doing so, I relive
that beautiful moment in time when we were so young and naive.*

*Linda, you are the love of my life; a gift from God. I am
so proud of how other women respect and look to you for spiritual
guidance. I deeply appreciate your love for the Father, your
compassion and service to people. I love how you set good examples
for our daughters and grandchildren. You are the best. Any man
would have been fortunate to have you as a wife. Thank you for
choosing me and sticking it out. I love you.*

Stan

One of the toughest things for me in writing this book
is knowing where to stop and how to end it. I believe I have
given a quite full and candid account of my life. I've been as
transparent as I can. I have done it because I want everyone
who reads this book to see they are not alone in the bad
choices they have made, the harm they have suffered as a
result, and the relationships they have damaged due to unwise
choices.

As Romans 3:23 states: "All have sinned and fall short of the glory of God." This means EVERYONE: you, him, her, all of us and me.

The good news follows in Romans 3:24-26 . . . "and are justified by his grace as a gift, through the redemption that is in Christ Jesus, whom God put forward as a propitiation by his blood, to be received by faith. This was to show God's righteousness, because in his divine forbearance he had passed over former sins. It was to show his righteousness at the present time, so that he might be just and the justifier of the one who has faith in Jesus."

The gospel is simple . . . Jesus Christ, in the form of a human, came to earth where He lived as a man for some thirty-three years, was tempted yet sinless, suffered vicious beatings, died a horrible death on a cross, was buried in a sealed tomb and raised again on the third day. If we have faith to believe this, confess Jesus as our Savior and ask to be forgiven of our sins, and then follow the teaching of the Bible, we will receive the benefits of spending eternity in heaven with God. There, we will suffer no more, cry no more and no longer be sick or sad. This sounds like a good deal to me and I hope that you would agree.

As I conclude this book, I want you to be reminded that we have no control over where we came from, whom we were born to, or the circumstances in which we were born, that is--our heritage. However, the good news is we do have control over our destiny, that is, our inheritance.

Our world is currently in turmoil like most people have not seen before. If we could all agree on the issues, perhaps all the chaos would be resolved. Sadly, this is unlikely to happen because Satan, whom I call the enemy, is a master of deception and strife. His goal is to destroy. I choose to leave it all in the hands of the Creator who will be victorious in the end. For me, the following quote by Billy Graham makes sense and gives me hope as well as a task to perform:

"It is the Holy Spirit's job to convict, God's job to judge, and my job to love."

Afterword

Obviously, I am a believer in Christ and the Bible, and I want you to also believe in Him, but don't just take my word for it. I encourage you to read the Bible yourself and ask God to reveal Himself to you. Should you need to talk to someone, seek out one of your friends, spouse, or sibling who is a Christian or contact a pastor. You can also email me at stanfaddis@gmail.com. God bless you.

Made in the USA
San Bernardino, CA
05 November 2015